Sicilian Dragon: Classical and Levenfish Variations

BATSFORD ALGEBRAIC CHESS OPENINGS

SERIES EDITOR: R.G.WADE

Sicilian Dragon:
Classical and Levenfish Variations

David Levy

1 e4 c5 2 ♘f3 d6 3 d4 cd 4 ♘×d4 ♘f6 5 ♘c3 g6:   6 ♗e2;
                                                 6 f4;

B.T. Batsford Ltd, *London*

First published 1981
© David Levy 1981
ISBN 0 7134 2744 2 (limp)

Typeset by W. Turner & Son Limited, Halifax

Printed in Great Britain by
Billing & Sons Ltd,
London, Guildford & Worcester
for the publishers
B. T. Batsford Limited
4 Fitzhardinge Street, London W1H 0AH

BATSFORD CHESS BOOKS
Adviser: R. G. Wade O.B.E.
Technical Editor: P. Lamford

Contents

	The Dragon	vi
	Preface	vii
	Bibliography	ix
	Acknowledgments	x
	Symbols	xi
1	Introduction and Sixth Move Divergences	1
2	Seventh Move Divergences	9
3	8 ♘b3	15
4	Classical: 8/9 ♕d2	24
5	Eighth Move Divergences	38
6	Alekhine's 9 ♗g5	42
7	Ninth Move Divergences	49
8	Maroczy's 10 ... ♘a5	60
9	Tartakower's 10 ... ♕c8	69
10	Levenfish - Introduction	78
11	Levenfish with 6 ... ♘c6	83
12	Levenfish with 6 ... ♗g7!	103
	Index of Variations	109
	Index of Complete Games	111

We are told that the Dragon Variation derives its name from the shape of the Black pawn formation which is reputed to bear a resemblance to the silhouette of a dragon. Whatever may be our opinion concerning this explanation the Dragon Variation certainly gives rise to an order of ferocity quite beyond common experience, and this is perhaps the best justification for its mythical appellation.

If I, like Solomon, . . .
could have my wish —

my wish . . . O to be a dragon,
a symbol of the power of Heaven — of silkworm
size or immense; at times invisible.
  Felicitous phenomenon!

'O to be a dragon' by Marianne Moore

Preface

The Dragon Variation of the Sicilian Defence is without doubt one of the most interesting, complex, double-edged and difficult openings to play as Black or to meet as White. In writing a monograph on such a popular variation, one is struck by the vast amount of material available both in the form of detailed surveys in various publications and in the hundreds of master games in which ideas, both old and new, are tried.

Before I started to write this book, I decided to omit nothing which could be of interest to the really serious theoretician, yet to try to set out the material in such a way as to avoid baffling the more casual reader. (R. G. Wade deserves full credit for suggesting the lucid classification system now being employed in all Batsford's theoretical monographs.)

Within each system I have given the most frequently played variations as main lines, even though they may not represent best play for both sides. Many variations are illustrated by a game (or games) so that the reader can follow the strategies involved from their inception to the conclusion. I have also tried to show how and why various lines have evolved in order to give the studious reader confidence that he is playing the correct move for the right reason. Those who make the effort to learn the bulk of the material contained herein will reap their rewards time and again over the chessboard, for in a sharp opening such as the Sicilian Dragon it is not only the ideas that are important, but also the numerous tricks, traps and devastatingly swift attacks that often seem to turn up as if from nowhere.

As the reader will see from the bibliography I have used many sources for my material. Most of them have been from my own library though I must thank R. G. Wade and L. W. Barden who made available to me a large amount of invaluable material which I did not otherwise have at my disposal. I would also like to thank all those, too numerous to mention, who supplied me with scores of games that they had played or witnessed. Washington devotee Daniel Glazier was helpful in pointing out improvements in various places and Larry Evans' excellent columns in *Chess Life and Review* were often useful. Above all I must thank R. D. Keene who went through the original script with a fine-toothed comb in order to correct any errors in my analyses and who contributed no small measure of original analysis in the Levenfish Variation.

The poem 'O to be a dragon' is printed by permission of Faber and Faber Ltd. of London and The Viking Press of New York from *The Complete Poems of Marianne Moore*.

If any readers have ideas, additions or amendments that they would like to offer, I would be very pleased to consider them for any future editions of this volume.

D.N.L.L.
London, September 1980

Bibliography

The following list of books and periodicals includes all publications which were frequently consulted during the compiling of material for this book.

BOOKS
Boleslavsky, *Sizilianisch*, 1971
Boleslavsky, *Drachenvariante Bis Paulsen*, 1977
Ciocaltea & Samarian, *Teoria Moderna a Deschiderilor in Sah (volume 1)*, 1967
Euwe, *Theorie der Schach-Eröffnungen* (volume 9), 1961
Evans & Korn, *Modern Chess Openings* (10th Edition), 1965
Gufeld & Lazarev, *Sitzilianskaya Zashita*, 1970
Koblencs, *Sitzilianskaya Zhashita*, 1955
Marović & Sušić, *Moderna Teorija Otvorenja*, 1967
Matanović, *Encyclopaedia of Chess Openings* volume B, 1975
Mikenas, *Sachmatai*, 1968
Pachman, *Semi-Open Games*, 1970
Panov & Estrin, *Kurs Debyutov*, 1968
Schwarz, *Die Sizilianische Verteidigung*, 1979

PERIODICALS
Archives (English, German and Dutch), *British Chess Magazine, Chess, Chessman Quarterly, Chess Life, Chess Review, Chess Life and Review, Informator, Shakhmaty, Shakhmatny Bulletin, Shakhmaty v SSR, Teorijski Bilten, The Chess Player* (and *The New Chess Player*).

Acknowledgments

The author wishes to thank the following for their help in preparing this book: A. A. Smith for transliterating copy into algebraic notation, A. Sutton for retyping the manuscript, L. J. Smart for preparing the diagrams, and W. N. Watson for proofreading and providing valuable suggestions.

Symbols

+	Check
=	Balanced position
±	Slight advantage for White
∓	Slight advantage for Black
±	Clear advantage for White
∓	Clear advantage for Black
±±	Winning advantage for White
∓∓	Winning advantage for Black
∞	The position is unclear
!	Good move
!?	Interesting move deserving attention
?!	Dubious move
?	Weak move
??	Blunder
1-0	Black resigned
0-1	White resigned
½-½	Draw agreed
Ch	Championship
Corres	Correspondence game
OL	Olympiad
C	Candidates
IZ	Interzonal
Z	Zonal
F	Final
½F	Semi-final
¼F	Quarter-final
W or B	Beside each diagram, indicates the player to move.

1 Introduction and Sixth Move Divergences

1 e4 c5 2 ♘f3 d6 3 d4 cd 4 ♘×d4 ♘f6 5 ♘c3 g6

Black's initial aim in the Classical Dragon is to reach the type of position shown in diagram 1 which we shall refer to as the 'normal position'. His pieces are then reasonably well developed, ready to rebuff any attack on the K-side or in the centre. In addition, he has every opportunity to create play on the Q-wing with the Dragon bishop, the semi-open c-file and the possible advances ... b5 or ... a5 - a4 being the most significant features of his plans.

Layout

After:

6 ♗e2

Sixth move alternatives form the remainder of this chapter.

6 ...   ♗g7
7 ♗e3

Other seventh moves are dealt with in chapter 2, except Alekhine's 7 0-0 ♘c6 8 ♘b3 0-0 9 ♗g5 which forms the subject of chapter 6.

7 ...   ♘c6
8 0-0

For **8 ♘b3** see chapter 3; **8/9 ♕d2** is chapter 4; while **8 Others** are covered in chapter 5.

8 ...   0-0
9 ♘b3 *(1)*

reaching the normal position. For other ninth moves see chapter 7.

All significant divergences within this sequence are due to White and they provide us with a convenient method of subdividing the Classical Dragon.

1
B

9 ...   ♗e6

Alternatives are dealt with in chapter 7.

10 f4

and now Black has the choice between Maroczy's **10 ... ♞a5** (chapter 8) and Tartakower's **10 ... ♛c8** (chapter 9). Some minor tenth moves are summarised at the end of chapter 7.

Sixth move divergences

The Levenfish Attack **6 f4** is considered in chapter 10 p.78.

We now consider:
A: 6 h3
B: 6 ♞de2
C: 6 ♗b5+
D: 6 ♞d5
E: 6 ♗g5
F: 6 g3

6 ♞b3 does no more than transpose to variations considered after 7 ♞b3, 8 ♞b3 or 9 ♞b3.

A:

6 h3 (2)

This idea of Lasker's prepares for an early sally on the K-side with g4, but in a position where White's development is far from complete such a plan should not be successful.

6 ... ♗g7
7 ♗e3

After 7 g4 a6 we would reach Fischer-Reshevsky, US Ch 1962-63, by transposition; it continued 8 g5!? (Fischer, in *My 60 Memorable Games,* also mentions 8 ♗g2 0-0 9 0-0 ♞c6 =) 8 ... ♞h5! 9 ♗e2 e5 (If 9 ... ♞c6!? 10 ♞b3) 10 ♞b3 ♞f4 11 ♞d5 ♞×d5 (To be considered are 11 ... ♞×e2 12 ♛×e2 ♗e6 and 11 ... 0-0 12 h4 f5 or here 12 ... ♞d7!? sacrificing a pawn.) 12 ♛×d5 ♞c6 13 ♗g4! ♗×g4 14 hg ♛c8! 15 ♛d1! ♞d4? (15 ... ♛e6 =).

7 ... ♞c6
8 g4 0-0

In Henkin-Chistiakov, Black played less actively: 8 ... a6 9 g5 ♞d7 10 ♗e2 ♛a5 11 ♛d2 ♞c5 12 ♖d1 ♗e6 13 a3 0-0-0 14 ♞×c6 bc 15 ♗d4 ♗×d4 16 ♛×d4 ♞d7 17 b4 ♛×a3 18 0-0! and White had good possibilities of attack against the black king.

9 g5 ♞e8

White has over-extended his position to such an extent that Black could already be assessed as having the advantage.

The alternative 9 ... ♞d7? allows White to maintain equality by 10 h4 ♛a5 11 f4 ♞×d4 12 ♗×d4 e5 13 fe ♞×e5 14 ♗e2 ♛b4 15 a3 ♛×d4 16

♕xd4 ♘f3+ 17 ♗xd4 Reti-Samisch, Kiel 1921.

10 h4 ♘c7
11 f4 e5!
12 ♘de2 ♗g4!

The famous game Lasker-Napier, Cambridge Springs 1904, went 12 ... d5?! 13 ed ♘d4 14 ♘xd4 ♘xd5 15 ♘f5! ♘xc3 16 ♕xd8 ♖xd8 17 ♘e7+ ♔h8 18 h5!! ♖e8! 19 ♗c5 gh 20 ♗c4 ef 21 ♗xf7 ♘e4 22 ♗xe8 ♗xb2 23 ♖b1 ♗c3+ 24 ♔f1 ♗g4 25 ♗xh5!! Returning the material to nullify Napier's attack. 25 ... ♗xh5 26 ♖xh5 ♘g3+ 27 ♔g2 ♘xh5 28 ♖xb7 a5 29 ♖b3 ♗g7 30 ♖h3 ♘g3 31 ♔f3 ♖a6 32 ♔xf4 ♘e2+ 33 ♔f5 ♘c3 34 a3 ♘a4 35 ♗e3 1-0. There is no defence to g6. This is one of the great classic games of chess.

After 12 ... ♗g4! Black has some advantage, analysis by Kaufmann.

A2:

6 ♘4e2 (3)

Opočensky's move; this involves the knight on d4 in a time-consuming manoeuvre via e2 and f4 to d5.

6 ... ♗g7
7 ♘f4

7 g3 transposes to A6.

7 ... ♘c6
8 ♗e2 b6
9 ♘fd5 ♘xd5

By exchanging a piece that has moved four times within the first nine moves Black obtains a great lead in development. 9 ... 0-0 would be inferior because of 10 ♘xf6+ ♗xf6 11 ♗h6 ♖e8 12 ♕d2 as in Spielmann-Davidson, 1932.

10 ed
Or 10 ♕xd5 ♗b7 =
10 ... ♘d4
11 ♗e3 ♘xe2
12 ♕xe2 e5 =

A3:

6 ♗b5+ (4)

White tries to solve an internal communications problem in that this bishop, if on e2, can be an obstruction to his queen.

1 Introduction and Sixth Move Divergences

Hence White exchanges it off. However the simplification also eases Black's problems.

6 ... ♗d7
7 ♗×d7+ ♕×d7! =

After 7 ... ♘b×d7 8 0-0 ♗g7 9 ♗e3 0-0 10 f4 ♖c8 11 ♕f3 Korchnoi-Moiseyev, USSR 1950, White has a little more space and better control of the centre.

A4:

6 ♘d5 (5)

A trappy move.

6 ... ♗g7!

Not:

a) 6 ... ♘×d5 7 ♗b5+ ♗d7 8 ed ♗×b5 9 ♘×b5 ♗g7 10 0-0 0-0 11 ♖e1 ♘d7 12 ♗g5 ♘f6 13 ♘c3 ♖c8 14 ♘e4! ±.

b) 6 ... ♘×e4? 7 ♗b5+ ♗d7 8 ♕e2 f5 9 f3 ♘c6 (or 9 ... ♘c5 10 b4 ♘ca6 11 ♘e6) 10 ♘b3 ♘c5 11 ♘×c5 dc 12 ♗f4 ♖c8 13 0-0-0 ♔f7 14 ♗c4 e6 15 ♘c7 ± Estrin-Hofbinder, USSR 1943.

7 ♗b5+ ♗d7
8 0-0 ♘c6 9 ♘b3 0-0 10 ♖e1 a6 (Black's lead in development gives him a very slight edge.) Estrin-Averbakh, USSR 1939, continued 11 ♗f1 ♖c8 12 ♗e3 ♘×d5 13 ed ♘e5 14 ♗d4 ♗f5 15 c3 g5! ∓.

A5:

6 ♗g5 (6)

In most variations of the Dragon this bishop is placed on e3 to support the knight at d4. 6 ♗g5 can lead to very sharp games with equally sharp counteraction from Black. The logical way for Black to neutralise White's plans is to develop veiled threats against White's knight by ... ♗g7 and ... ♘c6.

6 ... ♗g7
7 ♕d2

7 ♗b5+ accomplishes nothing after 7 ... ♗d7 8 ♕e2 0-0 9 0-0-0 ♕a5 10 ♖he1 ♖c8 11 ♘b3 ♗×b5 12 ♕×b5 ♕c7 13 f4 h6! 14 ♗×f6 ♗×f6 15 e5 de 16 fe ♗g5+ Grechkin-Moiseyev, Iskra Ch 1951.

Introduction and Sixth Move Divergences

7 e5?! de 8 ♘db5 ♘bd7 can only be good for Black.
 7... ♘c6
 8 0-0-0

The alternative plan is 8 ♘b3 seeking to minimise the power of the Dragon bishop. Rauzer-Kan, 10th USSR Ch 1937, went 8 ♘b3 0-0 (8 ... h6 9 ♗h4 between the same two players in the 1936 Moscow Championship leaves Black in difficulties, as 9 ... 0-0 allows 10 ♗×f6 weakening the pawns.) 9 0-0-0 ♗e6 10 ♔b1 ♖c8 11 f3 ♖e8 12 g4 ♘e5 13 ♗e2 ♘fd7 14 ♗h6? (Better is 14 h4 though Black obtains strong counterplay with ... ♘b6.) 14 ... ♗h8 15 h4 ♘b6 16 h5 ♘ec4 17 ♗×c4 ♘×c4 18 ♕h2 g5!! 19 ♖d3 ♗e5 20 ♕g1 f6 21 ♕×a7 ♕d7 22 ♕g1 (If 22 ♕a4 both 22 ... ♘×b2 and 22 ... ♗×c3 23 ♕×d7 ♗×d7 24 ♖×c3 ♘e5 followed by ... ♘f7 win.) 22 ... ♕c6 23 ♘d4 ♕b6 24 ♘b3 ♕a6 25 ♕c1 ♗f4 26 ♕d1 ♘e5 27 ♘e2 ♘×d3 28 cd ♖a8 29 a3 ♕b6 30 ♘bd4 ♗e5 0-1.
 8... 0-0

Central liquidation by 8 ... ♘×e4 9 ♘×e4 ♗×d4! (9 ... ♘×d4 permits the tactical stroke 10 ♘f6+ gf 11 ♕×d4 with pressure, Rauzer-Ragozin, USSR 1936.) 10 ♗b5 ♗g7 11 ♕e3 0-0 12 ♗×c6 bc 13 ♘×d6 ♕a5 14 ♗×e7 ♕×a2 (Ragozin) is also satisfactory for Black.
 9 ♘×c6

9 ♘b3 besides being treated by ... ♗e6 as in the game cited at 8 ♘b3, presents Black's QRP with a target as shown in Neishtadt - Bandutto, corres 1959, which continued 9 ... a5 10 ♗b5 a4 11 ♘d4 a3 12 ♘b3 ab+ 13 ♔b1 ♕b6 ∓.
 9... bc
 10 e5 ♘e8 (probably 10 ... ♘d5 is stronger) 11 ed ♘×d6 12 ♗×e7 ♕×e7 13 ♕×d6 ♕g5+ 14 ♕d2 ♕a5 15 ♗c4 ♖b8 16 ♗b3 ♗f5 with good attacking chances for the pawn. Rauzer-Kan, USSR 1936.

A6:

6 g3 *(7)*

This has long been regarded as an innocuous move but recently it has been undergoing something of a revival. Like other sixth move divergences it is best answered by rapid development.

6 ... ♘c6!
This is the easiest way to equalise.

6 ... ♗g4 is regarded as inferior, an important game being Adams-Suesman, Boston 1944, which went 7 ♕d3 ♕c8 (Reasonable alternatives are 7 ... ♘c6 or 7 ... ♘bd7) 8 ♗g2 ♗g7 (van Steenis-Vlagsma, 1946, went 8 ... ♘bd7 9 0-0 ♘c5 which might be playable.) 9 h3! ♗d7 10 ♗e3 with a bind for White.

After 6 ... ♗g4 **7 f3** has also been tried, e.g. in Boleslavsky-Geller, Zürich 1953: 7 ... ♗d7 8 ♗e3 ♘c6 9 ♕d2 ♗g7 10 0-0-0 (Also possible is 10 ♗g2 ♘e5 11 b3) 10 ... 0-0 11 g4 ♖c8 12 ♔b1 ♘e5 13 h4 (Comparisons can now be made with the attacks stemming from Rauzer's 6 f3.) 13 ... b5 14 ♗h6 ♗×h6 15 ♕×h6 ♖×c3!? 16 bc ♕a5 17 ♕e3 ♕a3 18 h5 b4 19 ♕c1 ♕×c3 20 ♕b2 ♖c8 21 hg ♕b2+ 22 ♔×b2 hg 23 a3? ba+ 24 ♔×a3 ♘×f3!.

6 ... ♗g7 is not so accurate as the text, though after 7 ♗g2 0-0 Black can still hold his own, e.g. **8 0-0** ♘c6 9 ♘b3 ♗d7 10 ♘d5 ♘×d5 11 ed ♘e5 12 ♘d4 ♕b6 13 c3 ♖ac8 14 h3 ♕c5 15 ♕e2 ♖fe8 16 ♖d1 ♘c4 (Barcza-Pachman, Prague 1954) 17 b3 ♘b6 18 ♗b2 ♘×d5 19 c4

followed by 20 ♗×b7 with equality.

Examples of bad plans for Black in this line are, after 6 ... ♗g7 7 ♗g2 0-0 **8 h3** ♘c6 9 ♘de2 (Korchnoi-Suetin, 31st USSR Ch 1963 went 9 ♘b3 ♗e6?! 10 ♘d5! a5 11 a4 ♘b4 12 c3 ♘b×d5 13 ed ♗d7 14 ♘d4 ♕c8 15 ♕b3 ♘e8 16 ♗e3 ♘c7 17 h4 and White has pressure along the central files.) And now:

a) Bronstein-Sajtar, Moscow-Prague 1946, went **9 ... a6** 10 0-0 ♘e5 11 ♔h2 ♗d7 12 f4 ♘c4 13 b3 ♘a5 14 ♗e3 ♖c8 15 ♕d2 b5 16 a3 ♕c7 17 ♖ad1 with a good position for White.

b) Korchnoi-Bondarevsky, Leningrad 1963, continued **9 ... ♗d7** 10 0-0 ♖c8 11 ♘d5 ♘d5 12 ed ♘e5 13 a4! ♘c4 14 ♖a2 e5 15 de ♗×e6 16 ♘f4 ♘a5 17 ♘d5 ♘c6 18 ♖a3! also with advantage for White.

c) Correct is **9 ... ♖b8** transposing to the Matanović-Gligorić game mentioned in the note to the next move.

An example of a bad plan for White is 6 ... ♗g7 **7 h3?!** ♘c6 8 ♘b3? ♗e6! 9 ♗g2 ♗c4 (now White cannot castle short) 10 ♗g5 0-0 11 ♕d2 b5! ∓ Ermenkov-Rajković, Vrnjacka Banja 1978.

7 ♗g2

1 Introduction and Sixth Move Divergences 7

White might also try 7 ♘de2, to avoid the possibility of the important exchange of knights on d4, e.g. 7 ... ♗g7 8 ♗g2 0-0 (not 8 ... h5?! 9 h3 h4 10 g4 ±; 8 ... ♗d7 equalizes, 9 0-0 ♕c8 10 ♘f4 0-0 11 ♖e1 ♖e8 12 ♖b1 ♘e5 Ciocaltea-Rajković, Belgrade 1979.) 9 0-0 but Black obtains easy equality with either
a) 9 ... ♖b8 10 h3 b5 11 ♘f4 b4 12 ♘cd5 a5 = Matanović - Gligorić, Yugoslav Ch 1951, or
b) 9 ... ♗d7 = 10 ♘d5?! (better 10 h3 =) 10 ... ♘×d5 11 ed ♘e5 ∓ 12 ♘d4 ♕b6 13 c3 ♖ac8 14 ♕e2 ♖fe8 15 ♖d1 a5 (intending ... a4 - a3) 16 a4 and now, instead of 16 ... ♖c4? Tal-Gufeld, USSR Team Cup 1974, 16 ... ♘c4 is correct, e.g. 17 ♗f1 h5! ∓ -Tal.
c) 9 ... ♗g4 10 h3 ♗d7 11 ♗e3 ♖c8 12 b3 ♕a5 = Palacios-N.N., Havana 1978.
7 ... ♘×d4
This simplifying move leads to a level game. A recent try to preserve complications was seen in Cirić - Velimirović, Vrnjačka Banja 1966, which went 7 ... ♗d7 8 ♘de2 h5!? 9 h3 ♕c8 10 ♗e3 ♗g7 11 f3 ♘e5 12 ♗d4 0-0 13 g4 ♘c4 14 b3 ♘b6 15 gh?! ♘×h5 16 ♗×g7 ♘×g7 17 f4 ♕c5 18 ♕d4 ♕×d4 19 ♘×d4 ♖ac8 20 ♘de2 ♘h5 21 ♖f1 ♖c5 22 0-0-0 ♖fc8 23 ♖f3 f5 ∓.
After 7 ... ♗d7 **8 0-0** ♗g7 9 ♘de2 0-0 10 h3 a5! (Weaker is 10 ... a6 11 ♘d5 ♘×d5 12 ed ♘e5 13 c3 ± Pripis-Belyavsky, USSR 1978.) 11 ♗e3 a4 = is another possibility.
 8 ♕×d4 ♗g7
 9 0-0
a) **9 ♗e3** 0-0 10 ♕d2 (Not 10 0-0? ♘g4 11 ♕d2 ♘×e3 12 ♕×e3 ♗e6 13 ♘d5 a5! 14 c3 ♖b8 15 ♖ad1 b5! ∓ Evans - Reshevsky, Havana 1952.) 10 ... ♘g4 11 ♗f4 =
b) **9 ♗g5** h6!? (9 ... 0-0?! 10 ♕d2 ± Zhuravlev - Krogius, Sochi 1977.)
 9 ... 0-0
 10 ♕d3
Or:
a) **10 ♕d1** ♗g4 11 ♘e2 ♗e6! 12 h3 ♘d7 13 ♘f4 ♗c4 14 ♖e1 a5 15 ♘d5 a4 16 a3 ♖e8 17 h4 h5 18 ♗g5 ♗×d5 19 ed ♗×b2 ∓ Sokolsky-Furman, 21st USSR Ch 1954.
b) **10 ♕d2** ♕c7 11 ♘d5 ♘d5 12 ed b5 13 a4 b4! 14 ♕×b4 ♖b8 15 ♕h4 ♗×b2 16 ♗×b2 ♖×b2 17 c4 ♗a6 18 ♖ac1 ♖fb8 19 ♖fe1 ♕c5 20 ♕f4 ♖8b7 21 ♗f1 ♖2b4 22 h4! Cuellar-Korchnoi, Stockholm 1962.
c) **10 h3** ♗e6 11 ♕d1 (11 ♕d3?? ♕c8! ∓∓ Zinn-Panchenko, Lublin 1977.) 11 ... ♕a5 12 ♘d5 ♗×d5 13 e×d5

♘d7 14 c3 ± Janosević - Martinović, Yugoslavia 1978.
10 ... ♗e6
11 ♗d2

Teschner-Tal, European Team Championship 1957, went **11 ♘d5** ♖c8 (Also 11 ... ♖e8 12 c3 ♕a5 13 ♗g5 ♗×d5 14 ed e5 15 ♗×f6 ♗×f6 ∓ Riemsdyn-Sosonko, Sao Paulo 1978.) 12 c3 ♖e8 (instead, 12 ... ♘×d5 13 ed ♗f5 14 ♗e4 ♗×e4 15 ♕×e4 ♗f6 is worth considering.) 13 ♗e3 (Sharper is 13 ♗g5! and if 13 ... ♘×d5 14 ed ♗f5 15 ♕d2!) 13 ... ♕a5 14 h3? (14 a4 is preferable, e.g. 14 ... ♗×d5 15 ed a6 =) 14 ... ♕a4! 15 ♖fe1 b5 and Black has the better prospects.

If **11 b3** d5! 12 ed (If 12 e5 ♘g4) 12 ... ♘d5 13 ♗b2 ♖c8 with a good game.
11 ... ♕c7
12 b3 a6
13 ♖ac1

With the idea of ♘d1 - e3 and c4.

13 ... ♖fd8
14 ♘d5 ♘×d5

15 ed ♗f5 16 ♗e4 ♗×e4 17 ♕×e4 ♗b2! 18 ♖ce1 ♗f6 19 c4 ♖ac8 20 ♖c1 ♕d7 21 ♗a5 ♖e8 22 ♗b6 e5! 23 de ♖×e6! 24 ♕d3 ♖ce8 25 ♗e3 ♕e7 26 ♖cd1 ♗b2 27 ♗d2 ♕c7 28 ♖fe1 ♗a3 29 ♖×e6 ♖×e6 30 ♖e1 (30 ♗c3) 30 ... ♗c5 31 ♖×e6 fe 32 b4 ♗b6 33 ♗f4 e5 34 ♗d2 ♗d4 35 ♗e3 ♗×e3 36 fe ♕c6 37 ♔f2 b5 38 cb ab 39 e4 ♔f7 ½-½ Keres-Gligorić, Zürich 1953.

2 Seventh Move Divergences

After **1 e4 c5 2 ♘f3 d6 3 d4 cd 4 ♘×d4 ♘f6 5 ♘c3 g6 6 ♗e2 ♗g7**

Close scrutiny is given to:

7 ♘b3 *(8)*

7 ♗e3 is, and 7 O-O can become, the main line of the Classical Dragon.

7 O-O O-O will transpose to other lines as follows:

a) **8 f4** ♕b6! 9 ♗e3 (9 ♔h1? ♘×e4) when:

a1) **9 ... ♘c6** is D, p.50.

a2) Also possible here is **9 ... ♕×b2** 10 ♕d3 ♕b4 11 e5 de 12 fe ♘g4 13 ♗×g4 ♗×g4 14 ♖f4 ♗d7 15 ♘d5 ♕a5 16 ♘×e7+ ♔h8 17 e6 ♕d8 18 ♖af1 with an interesting game, Belyavsky-Kupreichik, Kiev 1973.

b) **8 ♗e3** ♘c6 is the main line.

c) **8 ♘b3** ♘c6 reverts to the line being discussed.

If, after 7 O-O O-O, White avoids transposition into one of these lines he fares no better, e.g.:

d) **8 h3** d5! 9 ed (9 e5 ♘e4 10 ♘×e4 de) 9 ... ♘×d5 =

e) **8 f3** ♕b6! 9 ♔h1 ♘×e4!

10 ♘d5 ♘f2+ ∓

The text is an idea of Alekhine's which aims at early play on the K-side, omitting the move ♗e3 in the interests of saving time. Specifically, White's ♘b3 makes Black's counter ... d5 harder to achieve. Black's best plan is simple development and he must take care over the order of his moves.

7 ...   ♘c6

On 7 ... O-O:

a) **8 ♗e3** is harmless unless Black plays 8 ... b6? allowing 9 e5! ♘e8 10 ♗f3 ♘c7 11 ♗×a8 winning, as in Wright-Hartston, Cambridge 1968.

b) **8 O-O** transposes unless Black plays the inaccurate **8**

... ♗e6? ('Develop knights before bishops' — Emmanuel Lasker) allowing 9 f4 b5 10 ♗f3 ♕b6+ 11 ♕d4! ♗×b3 12 ♕×b6 ab 13 cb b4 14 e5! de 15 ♗×a8 winning, Matanović-Castaldi, 1951, whilst the passive 8 ... ♘bd7 permits White to establish a Q-side bind by 9 a4 a6 10 ♗e3 ♕c7 11 a5.

8 O-O

8 g4!? creates more dangers to White's king than to his opponent's; Smyslov-Korchnoi, Moscow 1960, continued 8 ... b6 9 f4 ♗b7 10 ♗f3 O-O 11 h4 a5 12 a4 ♘b4 13 h5 d5! 14 e5 ♘×g4! (=) 15 ♘d4 ♘h6 16 hg fg (16 ... hg 17 f5!) 17 ♘e6 ♕d7 18 ♘×f8 ♖×f8 19 ♘b5 d4 20 ♗×b7 ♕×b7 21 O-O ♘f5 22 ♘×d4 ♘×d4 23 ♕×d4 ♕c8 24 ♕e4 ♘×c2 25 ♖a2 ♕g4+ 26 ♕g2 ♕e6 27 b3 ♘d4 28 ♗e3 ♘f5 29 ♗f2 ♕×b3 30 ♖d2 ♕b4 31 ♖e2 ♕×f4 32 ♖e4 ♕d2 33 ♗×b6 ♕d5 34 ♖fe1 ♕c6 35 ♕a2+ e6 36 ♗f2 ♖c8 37 ♕b3 ½-½

If, instead of Korchnoi's logical 8 ... b6, Black plays the more natural looking 8 ... ♗e6, he comes under the full wrath of White's attack; 9 f4 ♖c8 (9 ... ♘a5 10 e5! ♘d7 11 ed!) 10 ♗e3 (or 10 f5 ♗×b3 11 ab O-O 12 g5 ♘d7 13 ♗e3 ♘c5 14 ♗f3 ♘e5 15 ♗g2 ±/± Kurajica-Martin, Malgret de Mar 1977) 10 ... a6 11 f5 ♗×b3 12 ab ♘e5?! (12 ... ♘d7 ±/±) 13 g5 ♘fd7 (better chances are offered by 13 ... ♖×c3!? 14 bc ♘×e4, though after 15 fg! hg 16 ♕d5 ♘c3 17 ♕×b7 ∞ it is still White for choice.) 14 O-O O-O 15 h4 ±/± Kurajica-Ivanović, Yugoslav Ch 1977.

8 f4 may transpose to 8 O-O O-O 9 f4, but another possibility is (8 f4) ♕b6, inhibiting K-side castling. Ornstein-Schutz, Stockholm 1978-9 continued 9 ♗f3 O-O 10 g4 ♗e6 11 ♘d5 ♗×d5 12 ed ♘a5 13 ♕e2 ♘×b3 14 ab ♘d7 ∓. White's attack is artificial and his king has nowhere safe to hide.

8 ...   O-O

8 ... ♗e6 is also satisfactory provided that Black replies to **9 f4** with **9 ... ♕c8** 10 ♗e3 (or 10 ♗f3 ♗g4 11 ♔h1 ♗×f3 12 ♕×f3 ♕g4 = Westerinen-Valvo, New York 1977) 10 ... O-O transposing to chapter 9 (see p.69), and not with **9 ... ♖c8** 10 f5 ♗d7 11 g4 ♘e5 (11 ... O-O was called for; now the black king is caught in crossfire in the centre) 12 g5 ♘g8 13 ♘d5 (±) 13 ... f6 14 ♗e3 b6 15 ♘d4 ♔f7 16 c3 ♕e8 (To meet 17 ♕b3 with ... ♗a4) 17 ♘e6! (threatening 18 ♘dc7) 17 ... ♗×e6 18 fe+ ♔f8 (If 18 ... ♔×e6 19 ♕b3 ♔d7 20 ♕a4+ ♘c6

2 Seventh Move Divergences 11

21 ♗g4+ causes congestion in Black's ranks.) 19 ♘×f6 ♘×f6 20 gf ♗×f6 21 ♗h6+ ♔g8 22 ♖×f6! ef 23 ♕×d6 ♖c6 (9)

9
W

24 ♕×e5!! de 25 ♖f1 ♖c8 26 ♗d1! ♖c4 27 ♗b3 b5 ♗×c4 bc 29 b3 a5 (Better is 29 ... cb 30 ab a5! e.g.: 31 ♖f3 ♕e7 32 ♔f1 ♕c5 33 ♔e2 ♕e7 34 ♔d3 ♕d6+ 35 ♔c2 ♕e7 36 ♔b2 ♕e8 37 c4 ♕e7 38 c5! ♕×c5 39 ♖f7 ♕d4+ 40 ♔a2 ♕d8! =; but perhaps White has better.) 30 bc ♕e7 31 ♔g2 ♕a3 32 ♖f2? (32 ♖f7 ♕b2+ 33 ♔g3 ♕×c3+ 34 ♔g4 ♕a3 35 c5! ♕×c5 36 ♖g7+ ♔f8 37 ♖c7+ picks up the queen.) 32 ... ♕e7 33 ♖f1 g5 (If 33 ... ♕a3 34 ♖f7) 34 ♖f5! g4 (Or 34 ... ♕d8 35 c5 ♕d2+ 36 ♖f2 ♕d8 37 c6 etc.) 35 c5 ♕d8 36 c6 ♕e7 37 c7 1-0, Gusev - Averbakh, Moscow 1951.

Another point of 8 ... ♗e6 in reply to 8 0-0 is that now 9 ♗g5 can be met by 9 ... ♘e5 (intending to occupy c4 or g4, possibly in conjunction with ... ♕b6+) e.g.; 10 f4 ♘eg4 11 ♗×f6 (What else? - if 11 ♔h1 ♘e3) 11 ... ♘×f6 ∓, Barclay-Watson, Glorney Cup, 1978. This move order, saving a tempo by not castling so early, may be a way for Black to by-pass the full force of Alekhinke's 9 ♗g5 (Chapter 6).

After 8 ... 0-0 White has:
A: 9 f3
B: 9 ♔h1
C: 9 f4

9 ♗e3 is again the normal position, for which see p.55.
9 h3 transposes into variation A p.49.

A:

9 f3 ♗e6 10 ♘d5 is an idea of Euwe's which is best answered by 10 ... ♗×d5 11 ed ♘b4 and, if 12 c4 or 12 ♗c4, 12 ... b5 would give Black good play.

B:

9 ♔h1

This is an interesting idea which effectively reduces Black's tactical possibilities along his a7 - g1 diagonal and prepares a K-side pawn storm by g4 supported by ♖g1.

9 ... a5!

This Q-side thrust, aiming for ... a3 in order to extend the range of the Dragon bishop and create play along the c-file, forces White to weaken himself by temporarily conceding b4 to Black's QN. Other moves are too slow, viz.:

a) **9 ... a6** 10 f4 (On 10 a4 ♗e6 11 f4 ♘a5 12 ♘×a5 ♕×a5 13 ♗f3 ♖ac8 14 ♘d5 ♘×d5 15 ed ♗d7 16 ♖a3 ±, Dolmatov-Hawelko, European Junior Ch 1979) 10 ... ♕c7 (10 ... ♗d7 11 ♗f3 ♖c8 12 ♗e3 ♕c7 - 12 ... b5!? - 13 ♘d5 ±, Parma-Velimirović, Yugoslav Ch 1978) 11 g4 e6 12 f5 ♖e8 13 ♗f4! ♘e5 (±) Alekhine-Foltys, Munich 1942.

b) **9 ... ♗e6** 10 f4 ♘a5 (Better is 10 ... ♕c8, e.g.: 11 ♕e1?! - correct is 11 ♗e3 with roughly equal chances; or 11 ♗f3 a5 12 a4 ♘b4 13 ♘d4 ♗c4 14 ♖f2 ♖d8 15 f5 d5! ∓, Dzieniszewski - Schneider, Jelenia Gora 1978 - 11 ... ♘b4 12 ♘d4 ♗c4 13 a3 e5 14 ♘f5 - if 14 ab ed - 14 ... gf 15 ab ♘×e4 16 ♘×e4 fe 17 f5 f6 18 ♖a3 ♗×e2 19 ♕×e2 d5 ∓, Westerinen-Saidy, Tallinn 1973) 11 ♗f3 (11 f5 ♗c4 12 ♗g5 ♖c8 13 ♗d3 b5 14 ♕d2?! b4! 15 ♘e2 d5! ∓, Larsen-Miles, Las Palmas 1978) 11 ... ♗c4 12 ♖g1 followed by g4 ±, König-A.R.B. Thomas, Bournemouth 1939.

c) **9 ... ♗d7** 10 f4 ♖c8 11 ♗f3 a6 12 ♗e3 b5 13 ♘d5 ♘×d5 14 ed ♘a5 15 c3 ♘c4

16 ♗c1 ±, Tessiz - Svacel, Prague 1959.

d) Panov recommends **9 ... b6** 10 f4 ♗b7 11 g4 ♘b4! 12 ♗f3 d5 14 e5 ♘e4 =
10 a4 ♗e6
10 ... ♘b4 is also satisfactory; Gebauer-Fred, Varna 1962, continued 11 g4?! b6 12 f4 ♗b7 13 ♗f3 ♖c8 14 ♗e3 ♘d7 15 ♕d2 ♖c4! ∓.

11 f4 ♕b6

Gufeld and Lazarev, surprisingly, fail to discuss 11 ... ♕c8 when the following possibilities arise:

a) **12 ♗f3** ♘b4 13 ♘d4 ♗c4 14 ♖f2 ♖d8 15 ♗e3 e5! 16 ♘db5 d5! ∓, Golak-Gufeld, Cheliabinsk 1959.

b) **12 ♗e3** ♗g4 13 ♗g1 ♖d8 14 ♘d5 ♗×e2 15 ♕×e2 ♘×d5 16 ed ♘b4 17 c4 ♕c7 18 ♘d4 ♖dc8 19 b3 ♘a6 20 ♖ae1 ♖e8 21 f5 ±, Alekhine-Golombek, Montevideo 1939.

12 f5

12 ♘d5 ♗×d5 13 ed gives Black an opportunity to obtain good play in the centre. Shatskes-Zakharov, Moscow 1961, continued 13 ... ♘b4 14 ♗f3 e6 (14 ... ♖ac8 15 c3 ♘d3 16 ♕×d3 ♕×b3 17 ♖e1 ±, Kurajica - Velimirović, Osijek 1978; but less accurate is 17 ♕e2 ♖fe8 18 ♗e3 ♕c4 19 ♕d2 ♘e4 20 ♗×e4 ♕×e4 ∓, Wilder-Ribo, Lone Pine 1979). 15 de fe 16 ♕e2 e5 17 c3

♘c6 18 ♕b5 ♕a7 19 ♖e1? ♕f2 20 ♗e3 ♕×b2 ∓.
12 ...   ♗×b3
13 cb   ♕b4
Not 13 ... ♕d4 14 ♕×d4 (Better than 14 ♗g5 =, Enevoldsen-Minev, Munich 1958) 14 ... ♘×d4 15 ♗c4! ±.
14 ♗e3   ♘d7
On 14 ... ♘×e4?? 15 ♘a2 wins the queen.
15 ♗c4   ♘b6
van den Berg-Larsen, Beverwijk 1959, continued: 16 ♘a2 ♘×c4!! 17 ♘×b4 ♘×e3 18 ♕e2 ♘×f1 19 ♘×c6 ♘g3+ 20 hg bc 21 b4! (Otherwise 21 ... c5 will leave White's two b-pawns as sitting ducks) 21 ... ab 22 a5 c5 23 ♖a2 ♗e5 24 ♕c4 ♗×g3 25 b3 ♖fb8 26 ♔g1 ♔g7 27 ♔f1 ♖a7 28 ♔e2 ♗e5 29 ♔f3 ♗d4 30 g4 g5 31 a6 ♗e5 32 ♖a4 ♔f6 33 ♔g2? (Aimless. More to the point would have been 33 ♖a2, preparing to bring the rook back into the game. Now Black can force a decisive K-side break.) 33 ... ♖h8! 34 ♕b5 h5 35 gh g4! Black can take advantage of the exposed position of White's king to accelerate the advance of his passed pawns. White's resistance from now on was hampered by severe time trouble. 36 h6? ♖×h6 37 ♕b8 ♖h2+ 38 ♔f1 g3 39 ♕×a7 g2+ 40 ♔g1 ♗d4+ 41 ♔×h2 g1=♕+ 42 ♔h3 ♗e5

0-1. Though this game is far from flawless, it illustrates some of the more useful ideas for Black in the Classical Dragon.

C:

9 f4 *(10)*

9 ...   ♕b6+!
The most active continuation. There are two other equalising alternatives:
a) **9 ... b5!** 10 ♗f3 and now:
a1) **10 ... b4** 11 ♘d5 ♘×d5 12 ed ♘a5 13 ♘d4 (Rauzer, who suggested 9 ... b5, only wrote of 13 ♘×a5 ♕×a5 14 ♖e1 ♗f6. Better, according to Gufeld, is 14 ... ♕c7! 15 a3 ♗f5 16 ♗e4 ♗×e4 17 ♖×e4 a5 =) 13 ... ♕b6 14 c3 bc 15 bc ♕c5 16 ♗e3 ♕×c3 ∓ Abramov-Fridstein, Moscow Ch 1949.
a2) **10 ... ♗b7** 11 ♗e3 a6 has been suggested by Euwe.
a3) **10 ... ♕b6+** 11 ♔h1 b4 12 ♘d5 ♘×d5 13 ed ♘a5 14 ♘×a5 ♕×a5 15 a3 ♗b7 16 ♖e1 ♗f6 and now, instead of 17 f5? as in Abramov-Chistia-

kov, Moscow Ch 1949, Chistiakov gives 17 ♗d2 ♗×d5 18 ab ♗×f3 19 ♕×f3 =.
b) 9 ... ♗e6 10 ♗f3 ♗c4 11 ♖e1 ♕c8 12 ♘d5 ♖d8 13 c3 b6 =.

  10 ♔h1 a5
  11 a4 ♗e6

This move order is more accurate than 11 ... ♘b4 because after 12 ♘d2! (instead of 12 ♗f3) 12 ... ♗e6 13 f5! Black no longer has the move ... ♗×b3 at his disposal and he must therefore submit to the passive retreat 13 ... ♗d7. Godes-Karaseyev, USSR Armed Forces Ch 1960, now continued 14 ♘c4 ♕c7 15 ♗e3 ♖a6 16 ♘b5 ♕d8 17 c3 ♘c6 18 ♕d3 ±.

  12 ♘d5 ♗×d5
  13 ed ♘b4
  14 ♗f3 ♕a6

Black is now threatening 15 ... ♘b×d5 and 15 ... ♘×c2.

  15 ♗e2

L. Steiner-Podgorny, Marianske Lazne 1948, went 15 ♖f2 ♕c4 16 ♖d2 ♖fc8 17 c3 ♘c2! ∓.

  15 ... ♕b6

with a likely repetition of moves.

3   8 ♘b3

1 e4 c5 2 ♘f3 d6 3 d4 cd 4 ♘xd4 ♘f6 5 ♘c3 g6 6 ♗e2 ♗g7 7 ♗e3 ♘c6
   8 ♘b3 *(11)*

11 B

As with ♘b3 on move 7 (p.9) this is an idea, popularised by Alekhine, in which White once again plays for a K-side attack by omitting a developing move - in this case 0-0. 8 ♘b3 attempts to thwart Black's counter-thrust ... d5. This variation became well-known through the game Alekhine - Botvinnik, Nottingham 1936 - certainly the most famous of all Dragon games. Fischer employed this line in his 1961 match with Reshevsky, and it was then extensively analysed in chess literature with the result that Black's defensive resources have been considerably strengthened.

The general idea of this variation stems from a Russian first-category player, P. Rabinovich.
   8 ...   0-0
   9 f4

9 0-0 ♗e6 simply reaches the 'normal position', see chapters 8-9.

9 g4?! is a ragged and unsuccessful attempt to accelerate the K-side attack. Black may counter with:

a) **9 ... a5** 10 g5 ♘d7 11 ♘d4 ♘b6 12 f4! d5! 13 ♕d2 and now, instead of 13 ... ♘xd4 14 ♗xd4 de 15 0-0-0, when White maintains the initiative (Keres-I. Rabinovich, Leningrad - Moscow 1939) Black should play 13 ... e5 ∓.

b) **9 ... ♗e6** 10 g5 (10 f4 is best transposing back into the column) 10 ... ♘d7 11 h4 ♘b6! 12 h5 ♘c4 13 hg fg 14 ♗xc4 ♗xc4 15 ♕g4 ♘e5 16 ♕h3 ♕d7! 17 ♕xd7 (If 17 ♕xh7+?? ♔f7 18 ♕h3

Rh8 19 Qxd7 Rxh1+ 20 Kd2 Nf3++!) 17 ... Nxd7 ∓ Bronstein-Goldenov, Kiev 1941.

c) 9 ... **d5!?** 10 ed Nb4 11 Bf3 Nxg4! was played in Wade-B. H. Wood, Nottingham 1946 and Ugrinović - Kažić, Yugoslavia 1966. The latter game continued 12 Bxg4 Bxg4 13 Qxg4 Nxc2+ 14 Ke2 Nxa1 15 Rxa1 Bxc3 16 bc Qxd5 when White had many weaknesses. Filipowicz-Trapl, East European Armed Forces Ch 1969 went instead 12 Bc5 Na6 13 Bd4 Nf6 14 Be5 Bf5 15 Nd4 Qd7 16 Qd2 Nb4 =

After 9 f4 Black's main decision lies between:
A: 9 ... Be6
B: 9 ... a5!
C: 9 ... Na5
D: 9 ... e5

A:

9 ...   Be6
10 g4?!

The Rabinovich Attack.

White can transpose into the solid lines arising from the normal position with 10 0-0 (see page 60) and in view of the results of the text move this is probably his best chance.

Other White 10th moves give Black no worries, e.g.:

a) **10 Qd2** Rc8 11 0-0-0 Nb4 offers Black good chances - Euwe.

b) **10 Bf3?!** Bc4! 11 Qd2 Rc8 12 Rd1 (12 0-0-0 would be much too risky, but better would be 12 Kf2 or 12 Ne2 d5 13 e5 Nd7 14 0-0 or 14 Rd1 =) 12 ... Qc7 and now:

b1) **13 Nd5?** Qb8 14 Nd4 Rfe8! 15 Kf2 Nxd5 16 ed Nxd4 17 Bxd4 Bxd4+ 18 Qxd4 Bxa2 and Black should win. Rauzer-Lisitsin, 8th USSR Ch 1933.

b2) **13 Kf2** followed by Rhe1 and Kg1 would have been better.

After 10 g4 Black has:
A1: 10 ... Na5!
A2: 10 ... d5?!
A3: 10 ... Rc8

10 ... Nd7? (intending ... f5) is inferior because of both:

a) **11 f5** Bxb3 12 ab Nc5 13 Bf3 e6 14 0-0 Ne5 15 g5 f6 16 Qd2 fg 17 Bxg5 Bf6 18 Bh6 ± Kliavin-Chekhover, ½-final 20th USSR Ch 1952.

b) **11 h4** f5 12 h5! Nc5 13 hg hg 14 gf gf 15 Qd2 fe 16 0-0-0 Nxb3+ 17 cb Rc8 18 Rdg1 Bf5 19 Bc4+ e6 20 Qh2 Qf6 21 Nd5!! ed 22 Bxd5+ Be6 23 Bxe6+ Qxe6 24 Rxg7+ Kxg7 25 Qh7+ Kf6 26 Rh6++, Niephaus-P. Schmidt, Saarbrücken 1950.

A1:

10 ...   Na5! *(12)*

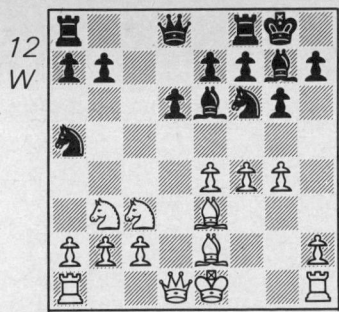

12 W

11 g5
11 f5 is not dangerous for Black providing that he continues:
a) not with **11 ... ♗c8** 12 ♘xa5! ♕xa5 13 0-0 ±, but
b) actively with **11 ... ♗c4** and now:
b1) **12 e5?!** ♗xe2 13 ♕xe2 ♘d7 (If 13 ... de 14 ♖d1 ♕c7 15 g5! wins a piece.) 14 f6 ef 15 ed ♘e5 16 0-0-0 ♘ac4 ∓.
b2) **12** ♘xa5 ♗xe2 13 ♕xe2 ♕xa5 14 0-0 ♖ac8 transposes into chapter 8, p.62.
b3) **12 0-0** a6 13 g5 ♘d7 14 ♘xa5 ♗xe2 15 ♕xe2 ♗xc3 16 ♘xb7 ♕c7 (Persitz-Pavitos, Ascona 1976) 17 bc! ♕xb7 18 ♗d4 e5 =.

After 11 g5 Black has:
A11: 11 ... ♘e8
A12: 11 ... ♘d7!

A11:
11 ... ♘e8
This is too passive.
12 ♗d4!
If 12 ♕d2 ♖c8 13 ♗d4 and

now:
a) **13 ... ♘c4** 14 ♗xc4 ♖xc4 15 0-0-0 ♕d7 16 ♕d3 gives White a good attack, Kan-Botvinnik, Moscow 1936.
b) **13 ... ♗c4!** (Botvinnik's suggested improvement) was tried in Louma-Alster, Bratislava 1948. White continued 14 ♗xg7 ♘xg7 15 ♗f3 ♗e6 16 0-0-0 ♘c4 17 ♕e2 ♕b6 18 ♖d3, when Filip has recommended the regrouping 18 ... ♘a5! 19 ♕g2 ♘c6 20 ♔b1 ♘b4 21 ♖3d1 a5 with a good game for Black.

12 ... ♗c4
Less active is 12 ... ♖c8 when Foltys-Eliskases, Podebrady 1936, continued 13 h4! ♘c4 14 ♗xc4 ♖xc4 15 ♕d3 ♖c8 16 0-0-0 ♕d7 17 ♖d2 ♗g4 18 ♘d5 b6 19 f5 e6 20 ♗xg7 ♔xg7 21 f6+! ♔h8 22 ♘e7 ♖d8 23 ♘d4 ♕a4 24 ♔b1 ♘c7 25 h5! gh 26 ♖dh2 ♕d7 27 e5! ♕xe7 28 ♖xh5 ♗xh5 29 ♖xh5 1-0.

13 ♗xg7 ♗xe2
14 ♕xe2 ♘xg7
Louma-Prucha, Brno 1944.
15 0-0-0
to be followed by ♘d5, when White will have a considerable spatial advantage as well as some attacking chances on the K-side.

A12:

11 ...   ♘d7
12 ♗d4   f6!

With White's king still in the centre, Black, by opening one or two lines, can easily create dangerous attacking chances.

The alternatives are:

a) **12 ... ♘×b3** 13 ab ♗×d4 14 ♕×d4 ♕b6 (Kliavin-Vetra, Riga 1952) 15 ♕d2 leaves Black no counter to the attack along the h-file.

b) **12 ... ♗×b3?** 13 ab ♗×d4 (13 ... e5 would have been much better) 14 ♕×d4 is very good for White because the adverse consequences of his spatial advantage (Black's attacking prospects against White's exposed king) have almost disappeared with the exchanges. Schories - Koch, 1933, continued 14 ... ♘c6 15 ♕d2 ♘c5 16 h4 a6 17 h5 b5 18 ♗f3 ♘e6 19 ♕h2 ♘cd4 20 ♗d1 ♘g7 21 hg fg 22 ♕×h7+ ♔f7 23 ♖h6 ♖h8 24 ♕×g6+ ♔g8 25 ♖×h8+ ♔×h8 26 ♕h6+ ♔g8 27 g6 1-0.

13 h4   fg!

Better than 13 ... ♘c6 and now:

a) White obtained a strong attack in Bronstein-Ragozin, 13th USSR Ch 1944. After **14 h5** fg 15 ♗×g7 ♔×g7 16 ♘d4 ♗g8 17 hg hg 18 ♘×c6 bc 19 ♕d4+ e5 20 ♕×d6 ♖f6, White could have kept his advantage with 21 ♕d3 followed by 22 ♕h3.

b) **14 ♗e3** also proved good in Foltys - Pelikan, Podebrady 1936: 14 ... ♘b6 15 ♘d4 ♘×d4 16 ♗×d4 d5 17 gf ef 18 ♗×b6 ♕×b6 19 ♘×d5 ♗×d5 20 ♕×d5+ ♔h8 21 0-0-0 ♖ad8 22 ♕b3 ♕f2 23 ♗d3!, when White was winning.

14 ♗×g7   ♔×g7
15 ♘d4   ♗g8
16 f5

So far Schubert - Pelikan, 1939. This is the only way to continue the attack since 16 fg would leave Black with the better game.

16 ...   ♕b6!

Not 16 ... gh 17 ♕d2 e5 18 fe ♘c5 19 ♘d5 ♘×e6 20 ♕c3 with a very strong attack for White.

Boleslavsky writes that Black must immediately embark on his counter-attack before White completes his development, and that after 16 ... ♕b6 he obtains good counterchances, e.g. 17 hg ♘e5 18 ♘d5 (18 b3 ∞ - Geller) 18 ... ♗×d5 19 ed ♕×b2 20 ♘e6+ ♔g8 21 ♘×f8 ♕c3+ 22 ♔f2 ♖×f8 and the white king is not to be envied his position.

A2:

10 ...   d5?!

This vigorous reaction in the

centre produces sharp positions that tend to favour the first player.
   11 f5
   Not 11 e5? d4! 12 ♘×d4 (If 12 ef ♗×f6) 12 ... ♘×d4 13 ♗×d4 ♘×g4 14 ♕d3 a6 followed by ... ♘h6 - f5 with an excellent game for Black, Levenfish - Botvinnik, Moscow 1936.
   11 ...   ♗c8
   Lipnitsky has recommended 11 ... gf in his *Voprosi Sovremennoi Shakhmatnoi Teorii* ('Questions of Contemporary Chess Theory'), 1954.
   12 ed
   12 fg transposes, after 12 ... hg 13 ed ♘b4 14 ♗f3, into the column, note to White's 13th move.
   12 ...   ♘b4
   13 ♗f3!
   Two extremely sharp alternatives are:
   a) **13 d6!?** ♕×d6! (Not 13 ... ed 14 g5) 14 ♗c5 ♕f4 15 ♖f1 ♕×h2 16 ♗×b4 ♘×g4 17 ♗×g4 ♕g3+ 18 ♖f2 ♕g1+ 19 ♖f1 ♕g3+ ½-½, Alekhine - Botvinnik, Nottingham 1936.
   b) **13 fg** is also inferior to the text in that prolonged tension cannot be maintained: 13 ... hg 14 ♗f3 and now:
   b1) **14 ... ♘×g4!** 15 ♗×g4 ♗×g4 16 ♕×g4 ♘×c2+ 17 ♔f2 ♘×a1 18 ♖×a1:

b11) **18 ...** ♖c8 19 ♗d4 ♖c4 (threatening ... e5) 20 ♖d1 b5 with counterplay - Sokolsky.
   b12) **18 ...** ♕d6 19 ♕g3 ♗e5 20 ♕h4 (More exact is 20 ♕h3) 20 ... ♖ac8 21 ♔g1 b5 22 ♘e4 ♖c4 23 ♘bd2 ♖a4 24 ♕h3 ♕×d5 25 ♘g5 ♖d8 26 ♖f1! ♗f6 27 ♘df3 ♖×a2? (27 ... ♔f8!) 28 ♕h7+ ♔f8 29 ♘e5! ♖×b2 30 ♘e6+! 1-0, Kramar - Kovalyev, Lvov 1947.
   b2) **14 ... e6!** 15 ♗c5 ♘f×d5 16 ♘×d5 ♗×d5 17 0-0 ♖e8 18 c4 (Sozin-Zhudro, corres 1937) 18 ... ♘f4 gives Black a comfortable game — Euwe.
   13 ...   gf
   14 a3!
   This is Pachman's recommendation.
   On 14 g5 there could follow 14 ... ♘g4 15 ♗c5 ♘a6 16 h3 (Not 16 ♗d4 e5! 17 de ♕×g5 Bondarevsky-Alatortsev, 10th USSR Ch 1937) 16 ... ♘e5 17 ♗d4 = - Keres.
   14 ...   fg
   Spassky-Listengarten, USSR Junior Teams Ch 1953, continued 14 ... ♘×g4? 15 ♗×g4 ♗×c3+ 16 bc ♘×d5 17 ♗h6 e5 18 h4 fg 19 ♗×f8 ♔×f8 20 c4 ♗e6 21 ♕e2! with a complicated game.
   15 ♗g2!?
   While this move is quite

strong, 15 ab, another Pachman suggestion, may be better, e.g. 15 ... gf 16 ♕×f3 ♗g4 17 ♕g2 ♗h5 18 ♗h6 (Pachman gave 18 ♗d4 ♗g6 19 0-0-0) 18 ... ♗g6 19 ♗×g7 ♔×g7 20 0-0-0. According to Boleslavsky White has the advantage.

15 ... ♘a3
16 ♕d3!

Pachman had recommended **16 ♕d2** followed by 0-0-0, but this is the very best queen move with which to prepare Q-side castling since it prevents the consolidating ... ♗f5-g3. After **16 ♕e2** ♗f5 17 0-0-0 ♕d7 18 ♘d4 ♗g6 19 h3, instead of 19 ... ♖ac8 as in Bastrikov-Rovner, Odessa 1951, 19 ... g3 would probably have given Black a tenable position.

16 ... e6

Or:

a) **16 ... ♘d7** when:

a1) **17 ♗d4?** ♘e5 18 ♕g3 ♕d6! 19 ♘e4 ♕c7 20 0-0-0 (Louma-Maximowitsch, Prague 1943) 20 ... f5 gives Black a tenable game - Euwe.

a2) **17 h3!** ♘e5 18 ♕e2 g3 19 0-0-0 and White has a similar position to the above Bastrikov - Rovner game but with the important difference that ♗d4 or ♗f4 will strengthen his attack while gaining a tempo on the knight.

a3) **17 0-0-0** ♘e5 18 ♕e2 leaves Black with a lifeless game according to Fischer. White has h3 and ♗d4 in the offing.

b) **16 ... ♕d6** 17 0-0-0 ♗d7 18 ♖hf1 ♖ac8 19 ♗d4 ♕×h2? (Correct is 19 ... b5) 20 d6! e5 21 ♖×f6! ♕×g2 22 ♗×e5 ♘c5 23 ♘×c5 ♖×c5 24 ♗d4 ♗×f6 25 ♗×c5 ♕f3 26 ♘e4! ♕×d3 27 ♘×f6+ ♔g7 28 ♘×d7! and White won after 28 ... ♕f5 29 ♗d4+ f6 30 ♘×f8 ♔×f8 31 d7 ♕×d7 32 ♗c5+ ♔e8 33 ♖×d7 ♔×d7 34 ♔d2 1-0 Nei-Pitksaar, Estonian Team Ch 1951.

17 0-0-0 ♘×d5

If 17 ... ed 18 h3 g3 19 ♗d4 is strong - Fischer.

18 h3! g3
19 ♖hg1 ♕d6!
20 ♗×d5 ed
21 ♘×d5?

21 ♗d4! is much stronger: 21 ... ♗×d4 22 ♖×g3+ ♗g7 (Or 22 ... ♔h8 23 ♕×d4+ f6 24 ♖f3 ±) 23 ♖dg1 ♕h6+ 24 ♔b1 ♗e6 25 ♖×g7+ ♕×g7 26 ♖×g7+ ♔×g7 27 ♕g3+ ♔h8 28 ♕e5+ and White is well on top - analysis by Fischer.

21 ... ♔h8

Fischer-Reshevsky, 2nd match game, New York 1961, continued 22 ♗f4 ♕g6 23 ♕d2 ♗×h3! 24 ♖×g3 ♗g4 25 ♖h1 ♖fe8 26 ♘e3 ♕e4? (A time trouble error. 26 ... f5! holds the balance, e.g. 27 ♕h2

♔g8) 27 ♕h2! ♗e6 (If 27 ... ♗f5 28 ♖×g7 ♔×g7 29 ♘×f5+ ♕×f5 30 ♘d4 wins - Fischer.) 28 ♖×g7 (28 ♘d2 is immediately decisive — A.R.B. Thomas) 28 ... ♔×g7 29 ♕h6+ ♔g8 30 ♖g1+ ♕g6 31 ♖×g6+ fg 32 ♘d4 ♖ad8 33 ♗e5 ♖d7 34 ♘×e6 ♖×e6 35 ♘g4 ♖f7 36 ♕g5 ♖f1+ 37 ♔d2 h5 38 ♕d8+ 1-0.

A3:
    10 ...   ♖c8
This has been generally regarded as incorrect.
    11 g5!
Not 11 f5 ♗×b3 12 ab d5! 13 ed ♘b4 14 ♗f3 ♘f×d5 15 ♘×d5 ♘×c2+ 16 ♔f2 ♘×a1 17 ♕×a1 ♖c2+ 18 ♔g3 ♗e5+ 19 ♔h3 e6 20 ♕d1 ♖×b2 21 ♘f4 ef 22 ♘d3 fg+ 23 ♗×g4 h5! 24 ♗×h5 ♕c8+ 25 ♗g4 ♕c3 winning. Dikarev - Kupreichik, Harkov 1965.
    11 ...   ♘d7
    12 ♕d2   ♘b6
Or 12 ... a6 13 0-0-0 ♘b4 14 ♔b1 b5 15 ♗d4 ♗×b3 16 cb e5 17 fe ♘×e5 18 ♗e3 ♕a5 19 a3 ♘bc6 20 ♘d5 ♕×d2 21 ♖×d2 ± Shmit-Bogorad, Riga 1966.
    13 0-0-0   ♘b4!
    14 ♔b1   ♘c4
    15 ♗×c4   ♖×c4
    16 ♗d4!   ♗g4

Estrin - Veresov, semi-final, Spartak TU Ch 1962, continued 17 ♖c1 ♗×d4 18 ♘×d4 ♕b6 19 ♘b3 ♖fc8 20 a3 ♘×c2! 21 ♕×c2 (If 21 ♔×c2 ♗f3 22 ♖he1 ♗×e4+ 23 ♖×e4 ♖×e4 with rook and two pawns and a continuing attack for two pieces.) 21 ... ♗e6 22 ♔a1 ♖×c3! 23 bc ♗×b3 24 ♕b2 ♖c4! 25 ♖b1 ♕a5 26 ♕×b3 ♖×c3 27 ♖hc1 and Black won after 27 ... ♖×b3 28 ♖×b3 ♔g7 29 ♖1c3 b5 30 h4 ♕b6 31 ♖e3 ♕d4+ 32 ♖bc3 a5 33 ♔b1 ♕d1+ 34 ♔b2 ♕g4 35 f5 ♕×h4 36 e5 de 37 fg hg 38 ♖f3 ♕d4 39 ♖fd3 b4! 0-1.

B:
    9 ...   a5! *(13)*

13
W

As we shall see, this move forces White to play into a variation of Tartakower's 10 ... ♕c8 (see chapter 9, p. 69) in which Black's chances are no less than equal.
    10 a4

After **10 a3** Black is able to create counterplay as in Konstantinopolsky - Averbakh, Moscow Ch 1950, by 10 ... a4 11 ♘d4 (If 11 ♘c1 e6!) 11 ... d5 12 e5 ♘e4.

Weaker is **10 0-0?** a4 11 ♘d2 a3 Henderson - Pilnik, Long Beach 1955.

10 ...   ♗e6

On 10 ... ♘b4 there are:

a) **11 ♗f3?** ♗g4! 12 ♗×g4 (If 12 ♖c1 ♗×f3 13 ♕×f3 ♘d7 14 0-0 ♖c8 15 ♘d4 ♘b6 16 ♘db5 ♘c4 ∓ Svensson-Bengtsson, Sweden 1978) 12 ... ♘×g4 13 ♕×g4 ♘×c2+ 14 ♔f2 ♘×e3 15 ♔×e3 ♕b6+ winning - Whiteley.

b) **11 0-0** ♘d7 12 ♗d4 e5 13 fe ♘×e5 14 ♘b5 ♗e6 with equality, Fichtl-Foltys, Prague 1943.

11 0-0!

Against **11 g4?** 11 ... d5 is very strong, the moves 9 ... a5 10 a4 helping Black to secure the use of his b4, e.g. 12 f5 ♗c8 13 ed ♘b4 14 fg hg and now:

a) **15 d6** ♕×d6 16 ♕×d6 ed 17 0-0-0 ♘×g4 18 ♗b6 ♗h6+ 19 ♔b1 ♘e3 20 ♖×d6 ♘×c2 ∓ Niephaus-Heinicke, 3rd match game 1951.

b) **15 ♗f3** ♘×g4! (15 ... e6 16 ♗c5 ♖e8 17 d6 ♘fd5! is also good for Black.) 16 ♗×g4 ♗×g4 17 ♕×g4 ♗×c3+ 18 bc ♘×c2+ 19 ♔f2 ♘×a1 20 ♖×a1 ♕×d5 ∓ with pressure against the knight - Euwe.

If **11 ♘d4** ♕b6! 12 ♘×e6 ♕×e3 13 ♘×f8 ♘g4! ∓ - Euwe.

If **11 ♗f3** ♘b4 12 0-0 ♘d7 13 ♘d4 ♗c4 14 ♖f2 e5! and now:

a) Matanović - Dimc, Zagreb 1953 continued **15 fe** de 16 ♘db5 with some advantage for White.

b) Bronstein - Korchnoi, Leningrad 1959, continued **15 ♘db5** ef 16 ♗×f4 ♗×b5 17 ab ♗e5 18 ♗×e5 ♘×e5 19 ♘a4 ♖c8 =.

11 ...   ♕c8

For 11 ... ♖c8 and 11 ... ♘d7 see chapter 7, variation E21, p.56.

12 ♗f3

12 h3! transposes into Tartakower's line, chapter 9, variation D, p.72, and 12 ♔h1 to variation A, p.69.

12 ...   ♘b4

Janošević - Vasyukov, Belgrade 1961, continued 13 ♘d4 ♗c4 14 ♖f2 ♕d8 15 f5 d5 16 e5 ♘e4 17 fg hg 18 ♘×e4 de 19 ♗g4 ♕c7 20 b3 ♗×e5 ∓.

C:

9 ...   ♘a5 *(14)*

This is yet another of the equalising lines at Black's disposal.

14 W

10 g4?!
White's best counter to ♘a5 seems to be 10 0-0 transposing, after 10 ... ♗e6, into the main line of the Classical Dragon. See chapter 8, p. 60.

10 ...   b6!

Black intends to combine pressure on the long white diagonal and on White's e4 with traditional play on the Q-side.

11 g5   ♘d7
12 0-0   ♗b7

van den Berg - Rajković, Orebro 1966, continued 13 ♗d3 ♖c8 14 ♘×a5 ba 15 ♕e1 ♘c5 16 f5 ♗e5 17 ♕h4 e6 18 f6 h5 19 ♗e2 ♔h7 20 ♗×h5 ♖h8! and Black had assumed the initiative.

D:

9 ... e5 is relatively unexplored. Pachman gives 10 0-0 a5 11 a4 ef 12 ♗×f4 ♖e8 13 ♗f3 ♘e5 =

4 Classical: 8/9 ♕d2

1 e4 c5 2 ♘f3 d6 3 d4 cd 4 ♘×d4 ♘f6 5 ♘c3 g6 6 ♗e2 ♗g7 7 ♗e3 ♘c6

There are two basically different plans behind White's ♕d2 on either the 8th or 9th moves, these being to:
a) Castle K-side and play along the d-, e- and f-files,
b) Castle Q-side with a wider range of possibilities of attack on the K-side (and sharper counter-attacks by Black).

8 ♕d2 *(15)*

15
B

8 0-0 0-0 9 ♕d2 is discussed under the transposition 8 ♕d2 0-0 9 0-0; see variation C, p. 26.

8 ... 0-0
8 ... d5 allows 9 ♗b5!

The main alternative is **8 ... ♘g4 9 ♗×g4 ♗×g4** when:
a) **10 0-0** 0-0 transposes into variation C4, p. 33.
b) **10 f4** ♗d7 11 0-0 also transposes into variation C4.
c) **10 ♘d5?** is trying for too much:
c1: **10 ... 0-0?** 11 c4 ♗d7 12 0-0 f5? (12 ... ♘e5 and if 13 b3 ♘g4! 14 ♗g5 f6 15 ♗h4 a6! preparing for ... b5 would have been much better.) 13 ef ♗×f5 14 ♘×f5 ♖×f5 15 ♖ad1 ♕d7 16 ♗h6 with advantage, Bogatyrchuk-Botvinnik, 8th USSR Ch 1933.
c2) **10 ... ♖c8** rebuffs White's plan:
c21) **11 c4** ♕a5 12 ♘c3 (the exchange of queens would also leave Black with a slight plus.) 12 ... 0-0 13 b3 ♗×d4 14 ♗×d4 b5! (∓) 15 ♘×b5? ♕×d2+ 16 ♔×d2 a6!
c22) **11 f3** ♗d7 12 c4 ♕a5 13 ♘c3 a6 14 ♖c1 ♘e5 15 b3 b5! ∓ Yeltsov-Chistiakov, USSR 1936.

After 8 ... 0-0 White has

the choice of:
A: 9 ♘b3
B: 9 0-0-0
C: 9 0-0

9 h3 would transpose into variation A, chapter 7, p.49.

A:

If White plays the non-committal **9 ♘b3** (which avoids the exchange of knights in variation B2) Black should continue actively with 9 ... ♘g4 (or 9 ... ♗e6 when Horowitz - Reshevsky, New York 1938, continued 10 ♗h6 ♗×h6 11 ♕×h6 ♕b6 12 ♕d2 ♖fd8 13 h3 d5 =), and now:
a) **10 ♗×g4 ♗×g4** 11 f3 (If 11 0-0 ♘e5 ∓) 11 ... ♗e6 =.
b) **10 ♗f4** (This saves the two bishops but loses time.) 10 ... a5! 11 a4 ♗e6 12 h3 ♘f6 13 0-0-0? (This does not fit in with 11 a4.) 13 ... ♖c8 14 ♔b1 ♘b4 15 ♘d4? (15 f3!) 15 ... ♖×c3! 16 ♕×c3 ♗a2+ 17 ♔c1 e5 18 ♗e3 ♘×e4 19 ♕e1 ed 20 ♗×d4 ♕g5+ 21 ♗e3 ♕e5 22 ♗d4 ♗h6+! 23 ♗e3 ♖c8 (23 ... ♕c5 24 ♗d3 ♘×c2! is more exact.) 24 ♗d3 ♗g7 25 c3 ♘×c3 0-1, Grechkin-Saigin, Sverdlovsk ½-final USSR Ch 1949.

B:

9 0-0-0 *(16)*

This is Grigoriev's move aiming for a quick bash on the K-

wing. Black has:
B1: 9 ... d5
B2: 9 ... ♘×d4
as well as 9 ... ♘a5 and 9 ... ♗d7.

B1:
9 ... d5

Black sacrifices a pawn in order to shift the emphasis of the struggle away from his own K-position to White's Q-side and into the centre.

10 ed
If 10 ♘×c6 bc 11 e5 ♘d7 ∓
10 ... ♘×d5
11 ♘×c6 bc
12 ♘×d5 cd
13 ♕×d5 ♕c7
Not 13 ... ♕×d5? 14 ♖×d5 ♗b7 15 ♖d7 ♗×g2 16 ♖g1 ♗h3 17 ♖×e7 ♗e6 18 a3 with a winning position.
14 ♕×a8 ♗f5
15 ♕×f8+ ♔×f8

Now, with **16 ♖d2** (Wade-Wotkowsky, Heidelberg 1949) or **16 ♗d3**, a position is reached which is almost identical to one in the Rauzer (Yugoslav)

Attack - see the companion volume *Sicilian Dragon: Yugoslav Attack* (Batsford). The difference here is that White has played ♗e2 instead of f3, and this gives him a marginally safer K-side set-up. The chances are about equal.

B2:
    9 ... ♘×d4
  10 ♗×d4 ♗e6

Also good is 10 ... ♕a5! 11 ♔b1 e5 12 ♗e3 ♗e6 =, this line being similar to variation C1 in *Sicilian Dragon: Yugoslav Attack* (p.39). The difference (White's e-pawn not being defended by a pawn) is to Black's advantage and White cannot play 13 ♕×d6? because of 13 ... ♖fc8! with the threat of 14 ... ♖×c3.

  11 ♔b1   ♖c8

The alternatives are less appetizing:

a) 11 ... a6 12 h4 b5 13 h5 b4 14 ♗×f6 ♗×f6 15 hg! hg! ± - not 15 ... bc? 16 ♕h6 ♖e8 17 ♕×h7+ ♔f8 (Broer-Vlagsma, Holland 1941) 18 ♗g4! ♗c4 19 ♖d5 and White wins.

b) 11 ... ♕c7 12 ♗f3! ♖fc8 13 ♖de1 ♘d7 (or 13 ... a6 14 e5! de 15 ♗×e5 ♕b6 16 ♕d4! ±) 14 ♗×g7 ♔×g7 15 ♘d5! ♗×d5 16 ed ♘f6 17 ♖e3 ♕d7 18 ♖he1 ♖c7 g4! ± Fuchs-Liebert, Halle 1961.

  12 h4   ♗c4
  13 ♗f3

Possibly better is 13 h5! ±
  13 ...   ♖e8
14 h5 ♕a5 15 a3 ♕a6 16 hg hg 17 ♘d5 e5 18 ♘×f6+ ♗×f6 19 ♗c3 (Smyslov-Konstantinopolsky, USSR 1945) 19 ... ♗e6 (threatening 20 ... ♕c4) 20 ♗e2 =

C:
    9 0-0 *(17)*

17
B

Tarrasch's continuation which is a great favourite of his apostle Unzicker. It is reached more frequently by the move order 8 0-0 0-0 9 ♕d2. The idea is to build up in the centre with ♖ad1 while avoiding committal moves.

Now we examine:

C1: 9 ... ♗d7
C2: 9 ... a6
C3: 9 ... d5
C4: 9 ... ♘g4

    9 ... ♘×d4 10 ♗×d4 ♗d7 will transpose to C1, but Black can play more actively on move ten with:

a) 10 ... ♗e6!? 11 ♖ad1 a6 12 f4 ♖c8 13 ♗f3 ♖c4 14 ♘e2 ♕c8 15 c3 b5 16 h3 b4 ∞ Petrosian-Getman, Spartakiad 1963.
b) 10 ... ♕a5?! 11 ♖ad1 ♗e6 12 ♗×f6 ♗×f6 13 ♘d5 ♕×a2 14 ♘×f6+ ef 15 ♕b4 ±

C1:
9 ... ♗d7

This move is too passive and allows White to implement his steady build-up.

10 f4 *(18)*

Black's passive 9th move allows White a wide choice of viable, though generally less impressive, alternatives:
a) 10 h3 a6 11 f4 b5 12 a3 ♖c8 is not so great for White.
b) 10 ♘b3 ♘e5 (10 ... ♖c8 11 ♗h6 ♗×h6 12 ♕×h6 ♘e5 transposes; while 10 ... a5 11 a4 ♘b4 12 f3 ♕c7 13 ♗d3 d5!? 14 ♗c5 de 15 fe ♘×d3 is also interesting, Rubinstein-Eliskases, Cordoba 1951.) 11 ♗h6 ♗×h6 12 ♕×h6 ♖c8 13 ♕e3 a6 14 h3 (Or 14 ♖ad1 ♕c7 15 h3 ♗e6 = Eliskases-Souza Mendes, Brazil 1944.) 14 ... ♘c4 15 ♗×c4 ♖×c4 = Bondarevsky-Szabo, Hastings 1960-61.
c) 10 f3 ♖c8 (Also possible is 10 ... ♘×d4 11 ♗×d4 ♗c6 followed by ... a6, ... b5,

and ... ♖c8) 11 ♖ad1 a6 12 ♘×c6 ♗×c6 13 ♘d5 ♗×d5 (Or 13 ... ♘×d5 14 ed ♗b5 15 ♗×b5 ab ± Goldstein-Purdy, Australia 1937) 14 ed ♘d7 15 c4 a5 = Djurasević-Pirc, Belgrade 1954.
d) 10 ♘×c6?! bc 11 ♗h6 ♗×h6 12 ♕×h6 ♖b8 13 b3 ♕a5 =/∓ Asztalos-Tartakower, Bled 1931.
e) 10 ♖ad1 (The most serious alternative.) 10 ... ♖c8 (It seems of little importance whether this move is played before or after ... a6, e.g. 10 ... a6 11 f3 ♖c8 12 ♔h1 b5 - *12 ... ♘a5 and 13 ... ♘c4 is also possible* - 13 ♘×c6 ♗×c6 14 a3 ♕c7 15 ♗h6 ♖fd8 16 ♗×g7 ♔×g7 = Ragozin - Korchnoi, 21st USSR Ch Kiev 1954. Weaker, however, is 10 ...♘×d4 11 ♗×d4 ♗c6 12 f3 ♖e8 13 ♔h1 ♕a5 14 ♗×f6 ♗×f6 15 ♘d5! ± Djurasević-Ivkov, Yugoslav Ch 1952.) 11 ♘b3 (11 f4 transposes to 10 f4 ♖c8 11 ♖ad1) 11 ... ♖e8 12 f3 ♕c7 (also possible is 12 ... ♗e6 13 ♘d4 ♘×d4 14 ♗×d4 a6 and ... ♗c4) 13 ♘b5 ♕b8 14 c3 a6 15 ♘a3 b5 ∓ Folz-Geller, Moscow OL 1956.

10 ... ♖c8

a) 10 ... a6 will normally transpose to the text.
b) 10 ... ♘×d4 11 ♗×d4 ♗c6 may be playable, e.g. 12

18
B

♗f3 e5 13 ♗f2 b5 14 ♖ad1 b4 15 ♘d5 ♘×d5 16 ed ♗b5 ∞ Nicevsky-D.Ilievsky, Skopje 1968, but not **11 ... b5?!** 12 e5! de 13 fe ♘g4 14 ♗f3 b4 15 ♗×a8 ± ± Penrose-J.Littlewood, Hastings 1961-2.

11 ♖ad1

a) **11 ♘b3?!** a6 12 ♗f3 ♗g4 =/∓

b) **11 h3** ♘×d4 12 ♗×d4 ♗c6 13 ♕e3 ♘d7 14 e5 de 15 fe e6 = Horowitz-Reshevsky, New York 1951.

c) **11 ♘×c6?!** bc 12 h3 ♕c7 13 ♖ab1 ♖b8 14 ♗f3 c5 = Czaja-Bogoljubow, 1937.

d) **11 ♗f3** a6 12 ♘b3 b5 (Also 12 ... ♗g4 13 ♔h1 ♗×f3 14 ♖×f3 b5 = Book - Reshevsky, Helsinki Olympiad 1952) 13 ♖f2 ♗g4 14 a3 ♗×f3 15 gf ♘a5 16 ♘×a5 ♕×a5 = Marini-Panno, Buenos Aires Ch 1953.

11 ... a6
12 h3

12 ♘×c6 ♗×c6 13 ♗f3 ♕c7 14 ♖f2 b5 15 ♘d5 ♕b7 16 ♗d4 is also marginally better for White. Pilnik-Pelikan, Mar del Plata 1944.

12 ... b5
13 a3 ♕c7
14 ♘b3 ♖fd8
15 ♗f3 ♗e8
16 ♕f2 ±

Unzicker - Eliskases, Saltsjobaden IZ 1952. White's game is slightly the more comfortable rather than superior.

C2:

9 ... **a6** (19)

19
W

This may transpose to some of the positions considered under C1, and like C1 the move fails to present White with sufficient opposition to his plan.

10 f4

a) **10 ♖ad1** ♗d7 transposes to note (e) to 10 f4 in variation C1.

b) **10 ♖fd1** ♗d7 11 f3 ♖c8 12 ♘×c6 ♗×c6 13 a4 a5 14 ♘b5 ♘d7 15 c3 ♘c5 = Bradvakević - Averbakh, Kislovodsk 1964.

c) **10 f3** ♕c7 followed by ... ♘a5, ... b5 and ... ♘c4, or

by ... ♘e5, ... ♗e6 and ... ♘c4, is perfectly satisfactory for Black.
10 ...   ♘xd4
10 ... ♗d7 leads to C1.
11 ♗xd4   b5
12 ♗f3   ♗b7
13 ♖ad1   ♕c7
14 e5   de
15 fe ±
Unzicker - Spanjaard, Luzern 1948.

C3:

9 ...   d5 (20)

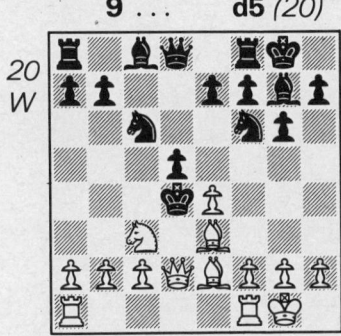

This liquidation of the centre carries the danger that White will be able to put his 3:2 Q-side majority to good advantage and that he will be able to put awkward pressure on the h1-a8 diagonal with ♗f3.
After 9 ... d5 White has a choice of:
C31: 10 ed
C32: 10 ♘xc6
C33: 10 ♖fd1

C31:
10 ed   ♘xd5

10 ... ♘b4 11 d6 e6 12 ♘db5 ♘bd5 13 ♗d4 ♘xc3 14 ♕xc3 ♘d5 15 ♕d2 ♗xd4 16 ♕xd4 leaves Black weak on the dark squares.
11 ♘xd5 (21)
a) 11 ♖ad1?! ♘xe3
b) 11 ♖fd1 and now:
b1) 11 ... ♘db4 12 a3 ♘xd4 13 ab e5 14 ♗xd4 ed 15 ♘b5 ♕e7 ∞ Hamann - Westerinen, Halle 1963.
b2) 11 ... ♘xd4 12 ♗xd4 ♗xd4 13 ♕xd4 ♘xc3 14 ♕xc3 ♕b6 15 ♕a3 (Or 15 a4 ♗e6 16 a5 ♕c6 17 ♕xc6 bc 18 b4 ♖ab8 19 c3 ♖fc8 20 f4 c5! = Kholmov-Spiridonov, 1976.) 15 ... ♗f5 = Szily - Ozsvath, Budapest Ch 1954.
b3) 11 ... ♘xe3! 12 ♘xc6 ♕xd2 13 ♘xe7+ ♔h8 14 ♖xd2 ♗xc3! 15 bc ♘f5 16 ♘d5 ♗d7 17 ♖b1 ♗c6 18 ♗f3 ♘h4 = Solmanis-Renter, 3rd Baltic Ch 1946.
b4) But not 11 ... ♘xc3 12 ♕xc3 ♘xd4 13 ♗xd4 ♗xd4 14 ♖xd4 ♕b6 15 h4! ± Solmanis-Beilin, 3rd Baltic Ch 1946.
c) 11 ♘xc6, as usual in the Dragon, strengthens Black's centre and gives him the possibility of counterplay along the b-file; after 11 ... bc:
c1) 12 ♘xd5? ♕xd5 (12 ... cd is also satisfactory) 13 ♕b4? ♗e6 ∓

c2) **12** ♖**ad1** and now:
c21) Smyslov-Denker, Groningen 1946, continued **12** ... ♗**f5** 13 ♘×d5 ♕×d5 14 c4! ♕e5 (Better is 14 ... ♕×d2 15 ♖×d2 ♖fb8 16 b3 a5 ±/= Cruz - Eliskases, Brazil 1944.) 15 b3 a5 16 ♗f3 ♕c7 17 ♗c5 ±.
c22) **12** ... ♕**c7** 13 ♗d4 e5 14 ♗c5 ♖d8 15 ♘e4 ± - Gufeld. If 15 ... ♗f5 or 15 ... f5 then 16 ♘d6! or if 15 ... ♗e6 16 ♕g5 threatening c4. In the game Timoshchenko-Belyavsky, Leningrad 1977, after 15 ... f5 White played the inferior 16 ♘g5 h6 17 c4 hg 18 cd cd. Play continued 19 ♕g5 ♗e6 20 ♗e7 ♖d7 21 ♗f6 ♗f7 ∓
c23) **12** ... ♗×**c3?!** 13 bc ♕a5 14 ♗h6 with a strong attack.
c24) **12** ... ♗**e6** 13 ♗d4! (weaker is 13 ♘×d5 cd 14 ♗f3. Szabo-Geller, Hilversum 1973 continued 14 ... ♕c7 15· ♗×d5 ♗×d5 16 ♕×d5 ♕×c2 17 ♖d2 ♕c7 18 b4 ♖ad8 19 ♕e4 ♖×d2 20 ♗×d2 ♕d7 =) 13 ... ♗×d4 14 ♕×d4 ♕b6 15 ♘a4! ♕×d4 16 ♖×d4 ±.
c25) **12** ... ♗**b7** 13 ♘a4 ♘×e3 14 ♕×e3 ♕c7 15 ♘c5 ♖ad8 16 ♗c4 ♗c8 ∞ Skold - Filipowicz, Leipzig OL 1960.
c3) **12** ♖**ac1** ♗e6 13 ♗d4 ♗×d4 14 ♕×d4 ♕a5 ½-½, Inkiov-Ristić, Smederevska Palanka 1978.
c4) **12** ♖**fd1** ♖b8 (Also playable are 12 ... ♕c7 13 ♗d4 e5 14 ♗c5 ♖d8 15 ♘e4 ♗e6 Rossetto-Iliesco, Mar del Plata 1945; and 12 ... ♗e6 13 ♗d4 ♗×d4 14 ♕×d4 ♘×c3 15 ♕×c3 ♕b6 = RodI - Heemsoth, Luneburg 1947) 13 ♗d4 ♗×d4 14 ♕×d4 ♕a5 (or 14 ... ♗f5 15 ♕×a7 ♖×b2 16 ♘×d5 cd = Shmid-Toran, Lugano 1959.) 15 ♕e5 ♕b4 = Bouwmeester-Matanović, Zevenaar 1961.

21
B

11 ... ♘×d4!
An important finesse. 11 ... ♕×d5? 12 ♗f3 ♕c4 13 b3 ♕a6 14 ♘×c6 bc 15 ♗h6! is good for White; Boleslavsky now gives 15 ... ♗×a1 16 ♖×a1 ♖e8? 17 ♕c3 e5 18 ♗×c6 with White finishing a pawn ahead.
After 11 ... ♘×d4 White has:
C311: 12 ♗c4
C312: 12 c4
C313: 12 ♗×d4

C311:
      12 ♗c4
A little artificial.
   12 ...   ♗e6!
Trifunović's solution. This is simpler than:
a) **12 ...   ♘f5** and now:
a1) **13 ♖ad1** ♘×e3! Schmahl-Carls, 1939.
a2) **13 ♗g5** ♗e6 14 ♘×e7+ (14 ♕b4 ♕c8!) 14 ... ♘×e7 15 ♕×d8 ♖f×d8 16 ♗×e6 fe 17 ♗×e7 ♖d2! ∓
a3) **13 ♗c5** e6! 14 ♘e7+ ♘×e7 15 ♕×d8 ♖×d8 16 ♗×e7 ♖d7 17 ♗a3 a6 = - Carls.
b) **12 ... ♘c6** 13 ♗c5 can transpose into a3).
   13 ♗×d4   ♗×d5
   14 ♗×g7   ♗×c4
   15 ♕h6   ♗×f1
   16 ♗×f8   ♕×f8
with complete equality, Honfi-Gufeld, Kecskemet 1958.

C312:
      12 c4
This move maintains the strong knight on d5, indirectly defends the b-pawn, and threatens the black knight.
   12 ...   e5!
12 ... ♘×e2+, exchanging Black's most active piece, must be suspect. After 13 ♕×e2 (threatening 14 ♗g5) 13 ... e6 14 ♘c3 b6 (if 14 ... ♗d7 15 ♖fd1 ♕c7 16 ♖ac1 ♗c6 17 ♘d5! with a strong initiative,

Krogius-Kots, Erevan 1962.) 15 ♖fd1 ♕e7 (Ilyin - Zhenevsky - Kan, Leningrad 1934, went 15 ... ♕h4? 16 c5! ♕b4 and now 17 c6 ±) 16 ♗f4 ♕f6 17 ♗d6 ♖d8 18 ♗e5! ♕g5 19 ♖×d8+ ♕×d8 20 ♖d1 ♕f8 21 ♗×g7 ♔×g7 22 ♕e4! ♗a6 23 ♖d7. White has a substantial advantage, Kirilov - Terpugov, USSR 1948.
   13 f4
After the continuation 13 ♖fe1? ♗e6 14 ♗×d4 ed of Stolyar-Taimanov, Leningrad Ch 1949, White has conceded Black the advantage of the two bishops and the better pawn formation.
   13 ...   ♗e6
   14 fe   ♘×e2+
   15 ♕×e2   ♗×d5
   16 ♖ad1   ♕e7!
Not 16 ... ♗×c4 17 ♕×c4 ♕c8 18 ♕×c8 ♖a×c8 19 ♖d7 ♗×e5 20 ♖×b7 (Geller-Averbakh, Szczawno Zdroj 1950) because White obtains an outside passed pawn and therefore the better ending.
16 ... ♕e7, suggested by Gufeld and Lazarev, guarantees full equality through Black's counterplay along the e-file.

C313:
      12 ♗×d4   ♕×d5
      13 ♖fd1   ♖fd8
      14 c3   ♗f5
Also possible is 14 ... ♗×d4

15 cd ♗f5 =, Skold-Pomar, Varna Olympiad 1962, and Fuchs-Szilagyi, Bad Liebenstein 1963.

15 ♗f3 ♗e4 = Johansson - O'Kelly, Varna Olympiad 1962.

C32:

10 ♘×c6

In *MCO*, 10th edition, Evans gives this move as being good for White, but his assessment can be challenged.

10 ... bc *(22)*

22 W

11 e5

This logical follow-up to White's previous move is stronger than 11 ♖ad1 **e6** 12 f4 ♕e7 13 e5 ♘d7, or, after 11 ♖ad1 Gufeld's suggested **11 ... ♕c7!** 12 ed cd 13 ♘×d5 ♘×d5 14 ♕×d5 ♗e6 with good counterplay.

11 ... ♘e4

This is the most active move, but possibly not the best.

a) **11 ... ♘e8** 12 f4 f6 should secure equality e.g.:

a1) **13 ♗f3** ♖b8! is analysed by Gufeld and Lazarev as being satisfactory for Black: 14 ♗×a7 ♖×b2 15 ♗d4 ♗f5 16 ♖fc1 fe 17 fe ♖b4 18 ♖ab1 ♖c4 19 ♖b7 ♘d6! 20 ♗b6 ♕e8 21 ed ♗×c3 22 ♗×d5+ cd 23 ♕×d5+ ♕f7 24 ♕×f7+ ♔×f7 25 ♖d1 ♖b4!.

a2) **13 ef** ef 14 ♗f3 (or 14 ♗c5 ♖f7 15 ♖ad1 ♘c7 16 ♘a4 ♘e6 17 b4 ♘×c5 18 ♘×c5 ♗f8 19 c4 ♕b6 =, Diez del Corral - Miles, Las Palmas 1978) 14 ... ♗e6 15 ♘a4 ♘d6 16 ♘c5 (if 16 ♗d4 ♗f7 17 ♘c5 ♘b5 18 ♗f2 f5 = - Koblencs.) 16 ... ♗f7 17 b3 ♕c7 and the threat to concentrate on e4 gives Black an even game, e.g. 18 ♖ad1 ♖fe8 19 a4 ♖e7 20 ♗f2 ♖ae8 = Bonch-Osmolovsky—Kopilov, USSR 1953.

Less satisfactory than the text are:

b) **11 ... ♘d7** 12 f4 e6 13 ♘a4 ±, e.g. 13 ... f6 14 ♘c5 ♘×c5 15 ♗×c5 ♖f7 16 ♕e3 Korn-Winter, London 1949; or 13 ... ♖e8? 14 ♕c3.

c) **11 ... ♘g4** 12 ♗×g4 ♗×g4 13 f4 f6 14 ♗d4 ♕a5 15 ♕e3 ♗f5 (Koblenz-Beilin, USSR 1947) 16 ♖f2 ± - Evans.

12 ♘×e4 de
13 ♕c3 ♕c7
14 ♗d4?!

It is better to protect the e-pawn with 14 ♗f4 because

after 14 ... ♗e6 15 ♖ad1
(Not 15 ♖fd1? f5! 16 ef ♕×f4
17 fg ♕×f2+ 18 ♔h1 ♖f6
∓) 15 ... a5 16 ♕c5! gives
White a positional bind - Gufeld.
Unless this can be improved on,
Black will do better with 11 ...
♘e8.
 14 ...   ♖d8
Black's threat to sacrifice the
exchange at d4 ensures him
adequate counterplay.
 15 ♖ad1
15 f4 is no better. Ravinsky-
Rovner, 1949, continued 15
... ef 16 ♗c4 ♖×d4 17
♕×d4 ♗×e5 18 ♔h4 ♗f6 ∓
 15 ...   ♗e6
 16 f4   ef
 17 ♗×f3   ♗d5 ∓
for, as Boleslavsky points out,
White cannot play 18 e6, because of 18 ... ♗×d4+ 19
♖×d4 ♗×e6 20 ♖×d8+
♕×d8 21 ♕×c6 ♕d4+ 22
♔h8 ♖c8 winning all of White's
Q-side pawns with ease.

C33:
 10 ♖fd1

As long as Black avoids the
trap that lies behind this move
he should have no difficulty
neutralising the position. The
other rook move, 10 ♖ad1,
can also be met by 10 ...
♘×d4 11 ♕×d4 ♘×e4! 12
♕×d5 ♘d6, e.g. 13 ♗f4 ♗e6
14 ♕c5 ♕c8 15 ♕a3 ♘c4 ∓,
Jul Bolbochan - Trumpowsky,
Rio de Janeiro 1938.
 10 ...   ♘×d4
Not 10 ... ♘×e4? 11
♘×c6! ♗×c3 12 ♕×d5
♕×d5 13 ♘×e7+ ♔g7 14
♘×d5 ♗×b2 15 ♖ab1 ♗e5
16 f4 ♗b8 17 ♗d4+ ♔h6 18
♗f3 f5 19 g4! with decisive
threats - Gufeld.
 11 ♕×d4
If 11 ♗×d4 ♘×e4 12
♘×e4 de 13 ♕c3 ♗×d4 14
♖×d4 ♕b6 15 ♖×e4 ♗e6
= Klovan-Shamkovich, USSR
1961.
 11 ...   ♘×e4!
 12 ♕×d5   ♘d6
 13 ♕f3
13 ♕b3 ♗b6 is no better for
White, Lisitsin-Kotkov, USSR
1956.
 13 ...   ♗e6
Vasyukov-Gufeld, 26th USSR
Ch 1959, continued 14 ♘d5
♘f5 15 c4 ♘×e3 16 ♘f6+
♗×f6 17 ♖×d8 ♖a×d8 18
♕×e3 ♗×b2 19 ♖d1 ♖×d1+
20 ♗×d1 ♖d8 21 ♗e2 b6 ∓

C4:   9 ...   ♘g4(23)

23
W

This move, gaining the two bishops at the cost of relinquishing some control of d5, has usually been the choice of Unzicker's opponents, and it may be the simplest way to equalise.

10 ♗×g4 ♗×g4

Of White's options in this position only the first three justify detailed examination.

C41: 11 f4
C42: 11 ♘d5
C43: 11 ♘×c6
C44: 11 h3
C45: 11 f3

C41:

11 f4 *(24)*

24
B

Richter's recipe. White hopes to embarrass Black's QB by the encircling threat f5. Black must play actively to maintain the balance, and best are:

C411: 11 ... ♗d7
C412: 11 ... ♘×d4

More passive alternatives are:

C413: 11 ... ♖c8
C414: 11 ... ♕a5
C415: 11 ... ♗e6

C411:

11 ... ♗d7

12 ♖ad1 ♖c8

If 12 ... ♘×d4 13 ♗×d4 ♗×d4+ 14 ♕×d4 ♗c6 15 b4 ♕b6 16 b5 ± Richter - Rellstab, Berlin 1938.

An interesting idea that was once in vogue in Czechoslovakia is 12 ... f5, to stem the advance of the White f-pawn. Two examples:

a) **13 ef** gf 14 ♖fe1 (or 14 ♕f2 ♖f6 15 ♘f3 ♖g6) 14 ... ♕e8 15 ♘d5 ♕f7 ∞ Foltys-Prucha, Prague 1943.

b) **13 ef** ♗×f5 14 ♘×f5 gf 15 ♖fe1 ♕e8 16 ♘d5 ♕f7 ∞ Foltys-Sajtvik, Prague 1943.

13 f5!?

One of Unzicker's theoretical contributions. Alternatives are:

a) **13 ♘d5** ♘×d4 14 ♗×d4 ♗×d4+ 15 ♕×d4 ♖×c2 16 f5 ♗c6 17 ♘e3 ♖e2! 18 ♘g4 h5 19 ♘h6+ ♔h7 20 ♘×f7 ♕b6! 21 fg+ ♔×g6 22 ♘e5+ de 23 ♕×b6 ab 24 ♖×f8 ♖×b2 25 ♖f2 ♖b4 26 ♖e1 ♗×e4 27 h3 e6 28 ♔h2 ♖a4 29 ♖e3 h4 30 g3 ♗d5 31 a3 b5! 32 gh ♖f4! ½-½. Richter-Petrow, Bad Harzburg 1938.

b) **13 ♖f2** ♕a5 14 h3 ♖fd8 (Threat 15 ... ♘×d4 16 ♗×d4 e5!) 15 ♕e2 ♘×d4 16 ♗×d4 when, instead of 16 ... ♗×d4 as in Trott - Stuart, Chester 1952, Gufeld suggests

16 ... ♗c6 to be followed by ... b5.
13 ... ♘e5
On 13 ... a6 14 ♘d5 e6 15 ♘×c6 bc 16 ♘b6 ± Unzicker-P. Schmidt, Bad Pyrmont 1950.
14 ♗h6 ♘c4
On 14 ... f6 15 ♘d5! is very strong.
15 ♕c1 ♘×b2
15 ... ♗×h6 16 ♕×h6 ♘×b2 is not good because of 17 ♖f3 followed by ♖h3.
16 ♗×g7 ♘×d1
17 ♕h6! ♘×c3
So far we have followed Unzicker - Giustolisi, Lugano 1959, in which after 18 f6 Black could have surmounted his immediate difficulties with 18 ... ef 19 ♗×f6 ♕×f6 20 ♖×f6 ♘×e4 21 ♖f4 f5! 22 ♖h4 ♖f7.
18 fg!
and White should win easily - Euwe.

C412:
11 ... ♘×d4!
12 ♗×d4 e5!
13 ♗e3
If 13 fe de 14 ♗e3 ♕×d2 15 ♗×d2 ♖ac8 =.
13 ... ef
14 ♖×f4
14 ♗×f4 ♕b6+ 15 ♔h1 ♕×b2 16 ♘d5 involves White in some risk. e.g. 16 ... ♗e6 17 ♗×d6 ♖fd8 18 ♖ad1 ♖×d6 19 ♘e7+ ♔h8 20

♕×d6 ♕×c2 21 ♘d5 ♕×a2. Barczay-Rigo, Hungarian Ch 1978 continued 22 ♘c7 ♖c8 23 ♕e7 ♗f8 24 ♖d8 ♖×d8 25 ♕×d8 ♔g8 26 ♘d5 ♕c4 ½-½.
14 ... ♗e6
15 ♖f2 ♗e5
Or 15 ... ♕a5 16 ♗d4 ♗e5 17 ♗×e5 ♕×e5 (also satisfactory is 17 ... de) 18 ♖d1 ♖fd8 19 ♕d4 ♕×d4 = Radulov - Estevez, Leningrad 1973.
16 ♗d4
Or 16 ♗f4 ♖c8 17 ♗×e5 de 18 ♕e3 = Pechan-Marsalek, Prague 1953.
16 ... ♖c8
16 ... ♕e7 17 ♖ad1 ♖fd8 turned out rather drawish in Matanović-Trifunović, Belgrade 1952. While 17 ♘d5 was shown to be no improvement in Philipp-Altrichter, East German Corres Ch 1978: 17 ... ♗×d5 18 ed ♗×d4 19 ♕×d4 f6 20 ♖af1 f5 21 ♖f3 ♖ae8 ∓.
One other possibility is 16 ... a6 17 ♘d5 (17 ♗×e5 de 18 ♕h6 and ♖ad1 may be better) 17 ... ♗×d5 18 ed b5 19 c3 ♖e8 ∓/∞ Mracek - Uhrovic, Corres 1977-8.
17 ♖d1 ♕a5
18 a3 ♖c4 =
Unzicker-Geller, West Germany-USSR 1960.

C413:

11 ... ♖c8 12 f5 ♗h5 13 h3 gf 14 ef ♗×d4 15 ♗×d4 f6 16 ♖ae1 ♗f7 17 ♖e4 ♔h8 18 ♖fe1 ♗g8 19 ♘e2 ♕d7 20 g4 ♕c7 21 ♕h6 ± Unzicker - Wood, Heidelberg 1949.

C414:

11 ... ♕a5 12 f5 gf 13 ef ♗×d4 14 ♗×d4 f6 (If 14 ... ♗×f5 15 ♕g5+ ♗g6 16 ♘d5 ♖ae8 17 ♖ae1 ♕d8 18 ♖×e7! ♖×e7 - 18 ... ♘×e7? 19 ♕f6! - 19 ♘×e7+ ♕×e7 20 ♗f6 followed by ♕h6 wins for White.) 15 a3 ♔h8 16 b4 ♕d8 17 h3 ♗h5 18 ♘d5 ♖c8 19 ♖ae1 ♗f7 20 ♘×e7 ± Foltys-Wood, Budapest 1948.

C415:

11 ... ♗e6 12 f5 and now:
a) **12 ...** ♗d7 13 ♘d5 ♖e8 14 c3 ♘e5 15 ♗h6 ♗h8 16 ♖f4 ♗c6 17 ♖af1 ± Engels-Iliesco, Mar del Plata 1941.
b) **12 ...** ♗c4 13 ♖f2 ♖c8 (If 13 ... d5 14 b3! de, as in Kohler-Kranki, Bad Oeynhausen 1940, White can win material by 15 f6!) 14 b3 ♗a6 leaves this bishop badly displaced.

C42:

11 ♘d5 *(25)*

This, the most active move, prepares to establish a Maroczy bind with 12 c4. If now 11 ... e6, 12 ♘c3 poses Black a

problem concerning his QB.
11 ... ♗d7
a) **11 ...** ♖c8 fails to reduce the force of 12 c4, e.g.:
a1) **12 ...** ♘×d4 13 ♗×d4 ♖×c4 which loses material to 14 ♗×g7 ♔×g7 15 ♘e3 ♖×e4 16 f3 ♖×e3 17 ♕×e3 ♗d7 18 ♕×a7 ± Kok - Spanjaard, Utrecht 1948.
a2) **12 ...** ♗e6 13 b3 ♗×d5 14 ed ♘×d4 15 ♗×d4 ♗×d4 16 ♕×d4 a6 17 a4 ± Taimanov-Ilivitsky, 16th USSR Ch 1948.
b) **11 ...** ♗e6 at once gives White too much space and all the advantages of the bind, e.g.: 12 c4 ♗×d5 13 ed ♘×d4 14 ♗×d4 ♗×d4 15 ♕×d4.

12 c4   ♘e5
13 b3   e6!

Euwe's idea. As compensation for his weak d-pawn, Black has active piece play.

14 ♘c3   ♕a5
15 h3

To prevent 15 ... ♘g4.

15 ...   a6
16 a4

Black was threatening to free his game with 16 ... b5. The alternative, 16 f4, also leads to equality after 16 ... ♘c6 17 ♘de2 ♖fd8.

16 ...   f5
17 f4   ♘f7
18 ef   gf =

Analysis by Boleslavsky.

C43:

11 ♘×c6 bc
12 ♗h6 *(26)*

26
B

This idea has been revived fairly recently in Cuba. The point is two-fold: White hopes to establish a Maroczy Bind by ♘a4 followed by c4 and b3; there is also the possibility that after 12 ... ♗×h6 13 ♕×h6 White may be able to attack on the ♔-side by advancing his f-pawn and bringing his rook to the h-file via f3.

Black's alternatives are:

a) 12 ... ♕b6? 13 ♗×g7 ♔×g7 14 ♘a4 ♕a6 15 b3 ♗e6 16 c4 with a strong bind, Lebredo - Levy, Cienfuegos 1972.

b) 12 ... ♗e6 13 ♗×g7 ♔×g7 14 b3 ♕a5 15 ♕e3 f5!? 16 ef ♗×f5 17 ♕×e7+ ♖f7 18 ♕e3 ♗×c2 with roughly equal chances, S. Garcia - Marović, Cienfuegos 1973.

c) 12 ... ♗×h6 13 ♕×h6 ♕b6 and if 14 ♘a4 ♕d4 15 b3 ♗e2 16 ♖fe1 ♗b5 ∓. White should try 14 ♕d2 ♕×b2 15 ♖ab1 ♕a3 16 ♖b7 when his well posted rook may compensate for the pawn.

d) 12 ... ♕a5 13 ♗×g7 ♔×g7 14 ♖fe1 ♗e6 15 ♖ad1 ♖ab8 16 b3 ♖fd8 = Sergeant-Landau, Hastings 1938/9.

C44:

Instead, hitting the bishop by **11 h3** merely wastes time because the purpose of h3 in the Classical Dragon is to prevent the exchanging manoeuvre ... ♘g4 which, in this case, has already taken place. After (11 h3) ♗e6! Black has retrieved his hold on d5 and his position is perfectly satisfactory.

C45:

On **11 f3** both 11 ... ♗d7 12 ♖ad1 ♖c8 13 ♖f2 ♕a5! 14 ♘b3 (Euwe-Denker, London 1946) 14 ... ♗×c3; and 11 ... ♗e6 12 ♘×c6 bc 13 ♗d4 f6! 14 ♘e2 (to prevent ... ♕a5) 14 ... ♕c7 are readily playable.

5 Eighth Move Divergences

After **1 e4 c5 2 ♘f3 d6 3 d4 cd 4 ♘×d4 ♘f6 5 ♘c3 g6 6 ♗e2 ♗g7 7 ♗e3 ♘c6** *(27)*

27 W

Now we examine:
A: 8 g4?
B   8 h3
C: 8 f3
D: 8 h4
E: 8 0-0 Miscellaneous

For **8 0-0 0-0** see Ninth Move Divergences, p.49.

For **8 ♘b3 0-0 9 0-0** see Ninth Move Divergences, p.55.

For **8 ♘b3 0-0 9 f4** see chapter 3, p.14.

For **8 ♘b3 0-0 9 g4** see chapter 3, p.14.

A:

8 g4?   d5
and now:
a) **9 ♗b5 ♗d7 10 ed ♘b4!** ∓.
b) **9 ♘×c6** bc 10 e5 ♘d7 11 f4 e6 12 0-0 0-0 ∓ Rödl - Müller, Bad Elster 1940.
c) **9 ed ♘×d5 10 ♘×d5 ♕×d5 11 ♗f3 ♕c4 12 ♘×c6** bc 13 b3 ♗c3+! ∓ - Euwe.

B:

8 h3
So as to play ♕d2 and 0-0-0 without fear of ... ♘g4.
8 ...   0-0
9 ♕d2
If **9 g4?** d5! 10 ed ♘×d5 11 ♘×d5 ♘×d4 12 ♗c4 ♗e6 13 ♗×d4 ♗×d5 14 ♗×g7 ♗×h1 ∓ Schories - Sämisch, Berlin 1920.

9 0-0 transposes to A, see Chapter 7, p.49.

9 ...   d5
and now:
a) **10 ed ♘×d5 11 ♘×d5 ♘×d4 12 ♘×e7+ (12 ♗×d4 ♕×d5 13 ♗×g7 ♕×g2** loses a pawn, Tartakower-Denker, Hastings, 1945-46.) 12 ...

5 Eighth Move Divergences

♕xe7 13 ♗xd4 ♗xd4 14 ♕xd4 ♖e8 15 ♕e3 (If 15 ♕d2? ♗f5 threatening 16 ... ♖ad8) 15 ... ♕xe3 16 fe ♖xe3 = - Euwe. e.g. 17 ♔f2 ♖e7 18 ♗f3 ♗f5 19 c3 ♖d8 20 ♖ad1 ♖ed7 21 ♖xd7 ½-½ Panchenko - Krogius, Sochi 1977.
b) **10** ♘**xc6** bc 11 e5 ♘d7 12 f4 e6 13 0-0 transposes into var. A, Chapter 7, p.49.

C:
8 f3 0-0 9 ♘b3 d5! 10 ed ♘b4 11 d6 ♕xd6 12 ♗c5 ♕xd1+ 13 ♖xd1 ♘c6 = Belavenets-Levenfish, Leningrad-Moscow 1939.

D:

8 h4 *(28)*

This move was employed by Smyslov in his 1958 World Championship match against Botvinnik. Now:
D1: 8 ... ♘g4?
D2: 8 ... 0-0
D3: 8 ... h5

D1:
8 ... ♘**g4?** denudes Black's K-side and gives White a good game after 9 ♗xg4 ♗xg4 10 f3 ♗d7 11 h5.

D2:
8 ...   **0-0**
This is rather risky.
9 h5
Tolush suggested 9 ♘b3 when Black would need to prepare ... d5 with ... ♗e6.
9 ...   d5!
Salhaazhuren - Stein, Budapest 1959, went 9 ... ♘xd4 10 ♗xd4 ♗e6 11 hg (if 11 ♕d2 ♕a5, threatening 12 ... ♘xe4, 12 ♖d1 ♖fc8 13 hg hg 14 f3 ♗c4 = Johansson-Akvist, Albena 1971) 11 ... hg 12 ♕d2 ♖e8 13 0-0-0 a6 14 ♖h2 ♕a5 15 ♖dh1 ♖ac8 16 ♕f4 g5 17 ♕f3 g4 18 ♕f4 ♘xe4 19 ♖h8+ 1-0.
10 hg
and now Black has a choice of two recaptures:
a) **10 ... hg**, and now:
a1) **11 ed** ♘xd5 12 ♘xc6 bc 13 ♘xd5 ♕xd5 14 ♕xd5 cd 15 0-0-0 ♗b7 (Alternatives here are 15 ... ♖d8 threatening ... d4 and 15 ... ♖b8 16 c3 ♗f5 17 g4 ♗d7 =) 16 f4 d4 17 ♗xd4 ♗xg2 (=) 18 ♖hg1 ♗e4 19 ♗xg7 ♔xg7 20 ♖d7 ♕f6 21 ♖d4 ♗f5 22 ♖gd1 ♖ac8 23 ♖1d2 ♖c7 24 b3 ♖h8 25 ♗c4! ♖h3 26

♔b2 ♖e3 27 a4 e5 28 fe+ ♔xe5 29 a5 ♗e6 30 ♗xe6 ♔xe6 31 ♖d8 ♔e7 32 ♖b8 ♖e6 33 c4 a6 34 ♘c3 f5 35 ♖dd8 f4 36 ♖e8+ ♔f6 37 ♖xe6+ ♔xe6 38 ♔d4 ♖f7?! 39 ♔e4! ♔d6 40 ♖b6+ ♔c5?? 41 ♔d3! 1-0 Smyslov-Botvinnik, Match (5) 1958.

a2) **11** ♘xc6! bc 12 e5! ♘e4 (Otherwise White quickly gets a terrific attack along the h-file.) 13 ♘xe4 de 14 ♗d4 when:

a21) **14** ... **c5** 15 ♗c3 ±

a22) **14** ... ♗e6 15 ♕d2 ♕c7 16 ♕f4 ♖fd8 17 ♗c3 ♗d5 18 ♕h4 ♔f8 19 0-0-0 e6 20 ♕f4 f5 21 ♕g5 ± Boyarinov - Pribilov, USSR Student Ch 1963.

a23) **14** ... ♕a5+ 15 ♗c3 ♕d5 16 ♕c1 ± - Botvinnik.

a24) **14** ... ♕d5 15 ♕d2 ♖d8 16 ♖d1 ♕xa2 17 ♕f4 ♕a4 18 e6 f6 19 ♕xe4 ± Galakhov - Ziyatdinov, Uzbekistan Ch 1977.

b) **10** ... **fg** 11 ed (11 ♘xc6 bc 12 e5 may be worth probing.) 11 ... ♘xd5 12 ♗c4! (Smyslov - Botvinnik, Match (7) 1958, went 12 ♘xd5 ♕xd5 13 ♗f3 ♕c4 14 c3 - if 14 ♘xc6 bc 15 c3 ♖b8! - 14 ... ♘xd4 15 cd ♗e6 16 ♕b3 ½-½; Black could now have tried 16 ... ♖xf3!? 17 gf ♕c6 18 ♕d1 ♗d5 19 ♖h3 ♕e6 with adequate counterplay - Model.) 12 ... e6 13 ♘xd5 ed 14 ♗b3 ♘xd4 15 ♗xd4 ♕e7+ 16 ♔f1 would be regarded as favourable to White - Botvinnik.

D3:

8 ... h5!
9 f3 0-0
10 ♕d2

If 10 ♘b3 ♗e6 followed by 11 ... d5 equalises.

10 ... d5
11 ♘xc6 bc
12 e5

Not 12 ♗h6 ♗xh6 13 ♕xh6 de 14 fe (Or 14 ♘xe4 ♘xe4 15 fe ♕d4! ∓) 14 ... ♕d4 ∓

12 ... ♘e8

On 12 ... ♘d7? both 13 f4 (e.g. 13 ... f6 14 e6 ♘b6 15 f5 winning) and 13 e6 (Botvinnik) are good for White.

13 f4

Not 13 ♗h6 ♗xe5! 14 ♗xf8 ♔xf8 as Black has good play for the sacrificed material.

An interesting new move is **13 g4!?** ♗xe5 14 0-0-0 hg 15 fg ♕d6 16 h5 ♘g7 17 hg fg 18 ♕d3 ♖f6 19 ♗d2 with a promising attack. Pereira - Pusenjak, ½-F 11th World Corres Ch.

13 ... f6
14 0-0-0

With this move White dissipates his initiative, and for this reason Botvinnik investigated the pawn sacrifice **14 g4!?** hg

15 0-0-0. It seems that when Black has such a good share of the centre he should be able to provide enough distraction to prevent White from continuing his attack; after 15 ... fe 16 fe ♕a5! the chances are about even.

14 ef ♘×f6 15 0-0-0 ♗f5 16 ♗d4 is devoid of any danger for Black.

14 ... fe

Smyslov-Botvinnik, Match (9) 1958, continued 15 fe ♗×e5 16 g4 ♗×g4 17 ♗×g4 hg 18 h5 g5! (Black must keep the rook's file closed at all costs.) 19 ♗×g5 ♕d6 20 ♖h4 ♘f6! (The tempting **20 ... g3** would be a fatal error: 21 ♖g4 ♔h8 22 ♗×e7! and White wins. **20 ... ♗f4** is not playable on account of 21 ♗×f4 ♕×f4 22 ♕×f4 ♖×f4 23 ♘e2 ♖a4 24 b3 ♖×a2 25 ♔b1 ♖a6 26 ♖×g4+ ♔h7 27 ♖g5 and Black's king will soon be in grave danger. Botvinnik states 'and Black has not a vestige of an advantage'.) 21 ♗×f6 ♕×f6 22 ♖×g4+ ♔h8 23 ♔b1 (If 23 ♖g6 ♗f4!) 23 ... ♖g8 (Not 23 ... ♖ab8 24 ♖g6! ♖×b2+ 25 ♔a1!!) 24 ♖b4 (24 ♖g6 leads to the better ending for Black after 24 ... ♖×g6 25 hg ♔g7 26 ♖h1 ♖h8 27 ♖×h8 ♔×h8 28 ♕h6+ ♔g8 29 ♕h7+ ♔f8 - Botvinnik.) 24 ... a5?! (24 ... ♖ab8! would have been much better, e.g. 25 ♖b3 ♖×b3 26 ab ♗f4 followed by ... e5-e4 with a good game for Black.) 25 ♖b6 ♗×c3 26 bc ♖ab8 27 ♖×b8 ♖×b8+ 28 ♔a1! ♖g8 29 ♕e3 ♖g4 30 a3 (Not 30 ♔b2? ♖b4+) 30 ... ♖e4 31 ♕d3 ♕e5 (31 ... ♕d6 is attractive but inferior because of 32 ♔b2 ♖a4 33 ♖a1 when White's king is quite safe.) 32 ♔b2 ♖e3 33 ♕d4 ♕×d4 34 cd ♔g7 35 ♖g1+ ♔f7 36 h6 ♖h3 37 ♖g7+ ♔f6 38 ♖h7 ♖h4 39 ♔c3 (Obviously not 39 ♖h8 ♖×d4 40 h7 because of 40 ... ♔g7 when Black wins.) 39 ... ♖h3+ 40 ♔b2 ♖h4 ½-½.

E:

8 0-0 h5?

Bird's continuation.

If 8 ... d5 9 ♗b5! ±.

9 h3

Not 9 f3 h4 10 ♕d2 ♘h5 11 ♘d5 e6 12 ♘c3 ♘g3 ∓ Reti-Breyer, Berlin 1920.

9 ... ♗d7

Tarrasch - Bird, Hastings 1895, continued 10 ♕d2 ♕c8 11 f4 ♔f8 12 ♖ad1 h4 13 ♘×c6 bc 14 e5! ±.

6   Alekhine's 9 ♗g5

No variation of the Classical Dragon has undergone such a transformation in recent years as Alekhine's attacking idea beginning with the move 9 ♗g5.
1 e4 c5 2 ♘f3 d6 3 d4 cd 4 ♘×d4 ♘f6 5 ♘c3 g6 6 ♗e2 ♗g7 7 0-0 ♘c6 8 ♘b3 0-0 9 ♗g5 (29)

29
B

White has delayed the development of this bishop until now so that it can be deployed on a more active square than the traditional e3. Amongst the ideas inherent in the text move are the conventional attack with f4, and the application of continuing positional pressure with an eventual ♘d5.

9 ♗g5 was played by Alekhine but it did not receive the mark of respectability until it was employed with success by the present World Champion Anatoly Karpov. At the time of writing (August 1979) this move is considered to be White's strongest weapon against the Classical Dragon.

Black's fundamental problem in this line lies in the difficulty of achieving adequate Q-side counterplay. We examine:
A: 9 ... ♗e6
B: 9 ... a5
C: 9 ... a6

9 ... ♖b8!? is an interesting idea that needs further testing. Lein-Shirazi, Tiruchirapalli 1978 continued 10 f4 b5 11 a3 a5 12 ♗f3 b4 13 ab ab 14 ♘d5 ♘×d5 15 ed ♕b6+ 16 ♔h1 ♘d4 ∞

9 ... ♗d7 is simply too passive. After 10 ♔h1 ♖c8 11 f4, Black is almost totally devoid of counterplay.

A:

6 Alekhine's 9 ♗g5

9 ... ♗e6 *(30)*

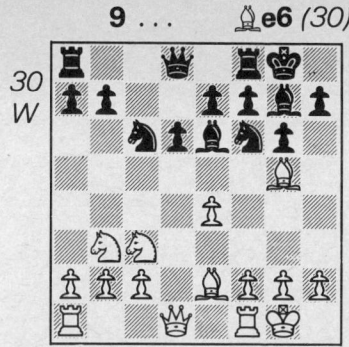

30
W

A1: 10 f4?!
A2: 10 ♔h1!

If 10 ♕d2 ♘a5 11 ♗h6 ♘c4 12 ♗×c4 ♗×h6 (Or 12 ... ♗×c4 13 ♗×g7 ♔×g7 14 ♖fe1 ♖c8 15 ♖e3 ♕c7 16 ♘d4 e5! 17 ♘f5+ gf 18 ♖g3+ ♔h8 19 ♕h6 ♘g4 20 ♖×g4 ½-½ Benko - Wexler, Buenos Aires 1960.) 13 ♕×h6 ♗×c4 14 ♖fe1 ♕b6 ∞ Kuzmin - Tseshkovsky, Minsk 1976.

A1:
10 f4?!

This move allows a tactical finesse based on the fact that the move ... ♕b6 is now check. Hence the preference for variation B, 10 ♔h1.

10 ... b5!

Possibly best, but other moves have also been played recently:
a) 10 ... ♘**a5** 11 f5 ♗c4 12 ♔h1 ♖c8 13 ♗d3 (13 e5?! ♗×e2 14 ♘×e2 - *14 ♕×e2 de 15 ♖ad1 ♕c7 16 ♗×f6 ♗×f6! 17 ♘d5 ♕c4* ∓ - 14

... ♘e4 15 ♘×a5 ♘×g5 16 f6 was played in one of the Dolmatov-Ristić games in the 1977 USSR - Yugoslavia match, and now, instead of 16 ... ♕×a5? 17 fe! ♖fe8 18 ed ♖b8 19 ♕d3 ♗e5 20 ♖ad1 ±, Black should have played 16 ... ef 17 ♘×b7 ♕e7 ∞, or 17 ... ♕b6 ∞) 13 ... b5 14 ♕e1! (Weaker is 14 ♕d2 b4 15 ♘e2 d5! 16 ♘×a5 ♕×a5 and now 17 ed?! ♗×d3! 18 ♕×d3 ♕×d5 ∓ Dolmatov-Ristić, USSR-Yugoslavia match 1977; or 17 e5 ♘e4 18 ♗×e4 de 19 f6 ef 20 ♗×f6 ♕d5 = Sigurjonsson-Sosonko, Wijkaan Zee 1977) 14 ... a6 (14 ... b4 15 ♘d1 d5 16 e5! ± Makarichev-Taborov, Daugavpils 1978) 15 ♘×a5 ♕×a5 16 ♘d5 ♕d8 17 ♗×f6 ♗×f6 18 ♘×f6+ ef 19 ♕h4 ♔g7 ∓ Zuyev-Taborov, Avangaard Ch 1978.
b) 10 ... ♕**c8** 11 ♕e1 (11 ♔h1 transposes to the main line.) 11 ... a5 12 a4 ♘b4 13 ♖c1 ♘×c2 14 ♖×c2 ♗×b3 15 ♖c1 ♕d8 16 ♕h4 with attacking chances for the sacrificed pawn. Bohosian-Minev, Bulgarian Ch 1974.

11 ♗f3

11 ♗×b5 ♕b6+ 12 ♔h1 ♘×e4 13 ♗×c6 ♘×c3 14 bc ♕×c6 15 ♗×e7 ♖fc8 16 ♕×d6 ♕×d6 17 ♗×d6 ♖×c3 18 ♖ac1 ♖ac8 19 ♖f2

♗f5 ∓.
11 ...   ♗c4
Or 11 ... ♖c8 = Alekhine-Schmidt, 1941.

12 ♖e1   ♖c8
13 ♔h1   ♘d7
14 ♖b1   a5
15 ♘d5   ♖e8
16 ♗g4   ♖b8 ∞

Bogdanović - P.Whitehead, Lone Pine 1978.

A2:

10 ♔h1! *(31)*

Now White is ready for f4, and Black must act quickly otherwise he will be slowly squashed.

10 ...   a5

This thematic thrust has been Black's most popular choice, but it is not at all clear that it is his best. Virtually all the other Dragon - line moves have been tried in this position but no firm conclusion should be drawn from the results of the encounters because White, almost invariably, has been the stronger player by far. Within the following possibilities there remains scope for a wealth of original ideas and analysis.

a) **10 ...♘a5** 11 ♘d5 ♗×d5 12 ed ♘e4 13 ♗c1 ♖c8 14 c3 (Or 14 ♗f3 ♘c5 15 ♘×c5 ♖×c5 16 ♖b1 ♘c4 17 b3 ♘e5 18 ♗e2 ±/± Lak - Hjartarson, Norway 1978) 14 ... ♘c4 15 ♗×c4 ♖×c4 16 ♕e2 ♕c7 17 ♗e3 b5 18 ♖ad1 ♖a4 19 ♘c1 ♕b7 20 f3 ♘f6 21 b3 ±/± Byrne-Martin, Las Palmas 1977.

b) **10 ... a6** 11 f4 b5 (Or 11 ... ♕c8 12 ♗f3 ♖b8 13 ♘d5 ± Bjork-Duchenne, World Junior Ch 1978.) 12 ♗f3 ♖c8 13 ♘d5! ♘d7 14 c3 ♘b6 15 ♕e2 ♘c4 16 ♖ad1 ♕d7 17 ♖fe1 ± Karpov-Martin, Las Palmas 1977.

c) **10 ... ♕c8** 11 f4 ♖d8?! 12 ♗f3 ♗c4 (Or 12 ... ♗g4 13 ♘d5 ♗×f3 14 ♕×f3 ♘×d5 15 ed ♘b8 16 ♗×e7 ♖d7 17 ♖ael ± Matanović.) 13 ♖f2 e6 14 ♖d2 ♕c7 15 ♕e1 h6 16 ♗h4 ± Karpov-Miles, Bad Lauterburg 1977.

d) **10 ... ♘d7** (Gligorić considers this move to be best.) 11 f4 ♘b6 12 f5 ♗c4 13 a4 a6 14 a5 ♗×e2 15 ♕×e2 ♘d7 16 ♖ad1 h6 17 ♗d2 ♘×a5 18 ♘×a5 ♕×a5 19 ♘d5 ♕d8 20 fg fg 21 ♘f4 ♕e8 22 ♘e6 ♖×f1+ 23 ♖×f1 ♖c8 24 ♕e3 ♗f6 25 ♕×h6 ♕f7 26 ♕h3 ♘f8 = Torre-Sosonko,

Bad Lauterberg 1977.
11 a4 &c8 *(32)*

32
W

Black has also tried, though without success:

a) **11 ... ♘d7** 12 f4 ♘b6 (After 12 ... ♗×b3 13 cb ♘c5 14 ♗c4 ♗×c3 15 bc ♘×e4 16 ♗h6 ♘f6 17 ♗×f8 ♔×f8 18 ♕f3 ♕b6 19 ♖ae1 ♖d8 20 ♗b5!, Black has insufficient compensation for the exchange. Matanović-Velimirović, Skopje 1976.) 13 f5 (Also possible is 13 ♘d2 ♖c8 14 f5 ♗d7 15 ♘c4 ♘×c4 16 ♗×c4 ♘e5 17 ♗b3 ♘c4 18 ♘d5 ♖e8 19 f6! ± Medina-de Francisco, Caracas 1977.) 13 ... ♗c4 14 ♗×c4 ♘×c4 15 ♕e2! ♘b6 (15 ... ♘×b2? 16 ♘d5 and c3, winning the knight; or 15 ... ♘4e5 15 ♘d5 ±) 16 ♕b5 ♘d4 17 ♘×d4 ♗×d4 18 ♖ad1 ♗g7 19 ♗e3! ♘d7 20 ♘d5 ± Karpov-Sosonko, Bad Lauterburg 1977.
b) **11 ... ♕c8** 12 f4 ♘b4 13 ♗f3 ♖d8 14 ♘d4 ♗c4 15 ♖f2 e5 16 ♘db5 ♕c5 17 ♖d2 ± H.Olafsson-Valvo, New York 1977.
c) There is also an interesting idea of Averbakh's which as yet is untested: **11 ... h6!?** 12 ♗h4 g5 13 ♗g3 d5 ∞.
12 f4 ♘b4
No other move has been tested in this position and the text does indeed look logical, now that White's a-pawn is on the fourth rank, but another possibility is 12 ... ♕b6, analogous to van den Berg-Larsen in variation B, (9 ♘h1) on page 13, e.g. 13 f5 ♗×b3 14 cb ♕b4, followed by ... ♘d7 and ♘f6.
13 ♘d4
13 f5 should be met by 13 ... ♗×b3 14 cb ♘d7 and not 13 ... ♘×e4?? 14 ♘×e4 ♗×f5 15 ♖×f5! gf 16 ♘g3 ±± Lein - Levy, Cienfuegos 1972.
13 ... ♗c4
14 ♘db5
This position was first reached in Platonov-Buslayev, USSR Spartakiad 1967, and for ten years no one could find a good plan for Black.
14 ... ♕b6
Interesting, but possibly insufficient, is 14 ... d5!?. Balashov-Geller, Lvov 1978, now continued: 15 ♗×c4 ♖×c4 16 ♗×f6 ♗×f6 17 ed ♕b8 18 ♕e2! ♖×f4 19 d6! ♖×f1+ 20 ♖×f1 ♕d8 21

♖d1 ±

15 ♗h4

In the original Platonov - Buslayev game White played 15 ♗×c4 ♖×c4 16 ♕e2 ♖fc8 17 ♖ad1 ♕c5 18 f5 and now Black rushed off towards e5 with 18 ... ♘c6?, overlooking 19 ♗×f6 ♗×f6 20 fg hg 21 ♘×d6! ±±. It remains an open question whether or not Black can improve on this and utilize his strength on the c-file to counter White's pressure in the centre.

The text is designed to embarrass Black's queen.

15 ...   ♗×e2

Feeble is 15 ... ♕c5 16 ♗d3 ♖fd8 17 ♗f2 ♕h5 18 ♗b6 ♕×d1 19 ♖f×d1 ♖f8 20 ♘a7 ± Karpov-Hernandez, Las Palmas 1977.

16 ♕×e2   ♕c5!
17 ♖ad1   ♕c4
18 ♖fe1   ♖fe8

Intending ... ♘h5

19 ♕×c4   ♖×c4
20 ♘a3   ♖cc8

Still intending ... ♘h5!

21 e5   de
22 fe   ♘g4
23 ♗g3   ♖ed8

After 23 ... ♘c6 24 ♘c4 ♘b4, it is not clear that White can do better than 25 ♘a3, with a draw.

24 h3   ♘h6
25 ♖×d8+ ♖×d8
26 ♗f2   ♘f5

27 ♖e4   ♖d2
28 ♔g1

Gaprindashvili - Belyavsky, Leningrad 1977.

28 ...   g5!

Much better than Belyavsky's 28 ... ♘c6? 29 g4!

29 ♔f1! ∞

If 29 g4 ♘h4 30 ♘c4 ♖×c2 31 ♘×a5 ♖×b2 ∓ - Tukmakov.

B:

9 ...   a5 (33)

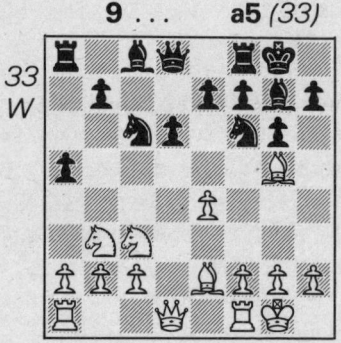

This move may transpose into variation A, but it has an independent significance for two reasons: White's f4 may not, after a4, be answered by ... b5; and secondly, Black may choose not to develop his c8 bishop on e6.

10 a4

This must be best.

10 ...   ♘b4

10 ... ♗e6 11 ♔h1 transposes to A, while 11 ♕d2 can be met by 11 ... ♖c8 12 ♖ad1 ♘e5! 13 ♘d4 ♗c4 14 ♘db5 ♗×b5! 15 ab ♕c7 =

6 Alekhine's 9 ♗g5

Vitolins - Georgadze, USSR 1976.

11 f4

The natural move. Vasyukov-Gufeld, USSR 1975, went 11 ♖e1 ♗e6 12 ♘d4 ♖c8 13 ♘×e6 fe 14 ♖a3 ♔h8 15 h4 ♕e8 ∞.

11 ...   ♗e6
12 f5   ♗d7

Here Black cannot try Larsen's idea, 12 ... ♗×b3 13 cb ♕b6+ 14 ♔h1 ♕b4 because the b4 square is already occupied.

13 ♘d4 ±/±

White has an ideal position. Buturin-Boidman, USSR Armed Forces Ch 1978, continued: 13 ... ♖c8 14 ♗e3 d5 15 e5 ♘e4 16 fg hg 17 ♘f3 ♘×c3 18 bc ♖×c3 19 ♗d2 ♖c8 20 ♕e1 ♗g4 21 ♕h4 ♕b6+ 22 ♔h1 ♗×f3 23 ♖×f3 ♖×c2 24 ♖h3 ±/±±.

C:

9 ...   a6 *(34)*

An idea of Gufeld's, aimed at a rapid ... b5 with immediate counterplay. As in variation B, the c8 bishop waits at home until its best square has been decided.

10 f4

10 a4 ♗e6 11 f4 ♘a5 (The difference - with no pawn on a5 Black can use the square for his knight.) 12 ♔h1 ♖c8 13 f5 ♗×b3 14 cb ♖×c3! 15 bc ♘×e4 16 f6 ef 17 ♗f4 ♘×c3 18 ♕d3 f5 ∞ Dolmatov - Gufeld, USSR 1978.

10 ...   b5
11 ♗f3   b4!

11 ... ♗b7 12 ♔h1 (12 ♘d5!?) 12 ... ♘d7 is also playable, but less forceful: Tal-Gufeld, USSR 1977, continued: 13 ♕e1 (13 a3 ♘b6 =) 13 ... a5! 14 ♘×b5 a4 15 ♘d2 h6 16 ♗h4 ♘c5! 17 ♘c4 ♗a6 18 ♘ba3 ♘d4!, and Black has more than enough for the pawn.

12 ♘a4
12 ♘d5 ♘×d5 13 ed ♘a5! ∓ - Gufeld.

12 ...   ♗d7!
13 a3
13 e5 ♘e8 ∓.
13 ...   ♖b8 ∓
14 ab   ♘×b4
15 ♔h1
15 e5 de 16 ♘ac5 e4!? ∞.
15 ...   ♕c7

Also possible is 15 ... ♗b5 16 ♖e1 ♕c7 17 ♘c3 ♗c4.
16 ♘c3   ♗e6
17 ♘a5

Or 17 ♘d4 ♗c4 18 ♖e1 e5! ∓.
17 ...   ♖fd8!
18 ♕e2   d5
19 ed
19 e5 d4! ∓.
19 ...   ♘f×d5
20 ♘×d5 ♘×d5

21 c3   ♖b5! ∓∓
Gofshtein - Gufeld, USSR 1978.

From the little evidence available, 9 ... a6 would currently appear to be Black's best reply to 9 ♗g5.

7 Ninth Move Divergences

After **1 e4 c5 2 ♘f3 d6 3 d4 cd 4 ♘xd4 ♘f6 5 ♘c3 g6 6 ♗e2 ♗g7 7 ♗e3 ♘c6 8 0-0**

8 ... 0-0

35
W

White has:
A: 9 h3
B: 9 f3
C: 9 ♔h1
D: 9 f4
E: 9 ♘b3

For 9 ♕d2 see Chapter 4, p. 26.

The first three variations (9 h3, 9 f3 and 9 ♔h1) are insipid moves, each of which may be countered by liquidating the centre with ... d5.

A:

9 h3 d5!

Smyslov-Geller, USSR Team Cup 1974, went 9 ... ♗d7 10 ♘b3 a5 11 a4 ♘b4 (cf. E2, especially the note to Black's tenth move) 12 ♗f3?! (better 12 f4 ♗c6 13 ♗f3 with an unclear position) 12 ... ♗e6! (if 12 ... ♗c6 13 ♘d5 ±) 13 ♘d4 (now if 13 ♘d5 ♘fxd5 14 ed ♗f5) 13 ... ♗c4 14 ♖e1 (14 ♗e2 immediately is probably good enough for equality) 14 ... ♖c8 15 ♗e2 d5!? 16 e5 (if 16 ed ♘fxd5 17 ♘xd5 ♘xd5 with an unclear position - Geller) 16 ... ♘e4 ∓ 17 ♗g4 e6 18 f4 ♘xc3 19 bc ♘a6 20 ♘xe6? (The combination is unsound. White should play 20 ♘b5!? ♗xb5 21 ab ♘c5 22 c4) 20 ... fe 21 ♗xe6+ ♔h8 22 ♗xc8 ♕xc8 ∓ White has at least material equality but he has too many weaknesses - especially on the white squares and along the f-file - which Geller exploits brilliantly: 23 ♕d4 ♘c7 24 ♕c5 ♕d7 25 ♕xa5?! (25

♖ab1!?) 25 ... ♘e6 26 ♖ab1 ♕f7 27 ♕a7 ♗a6 28 ♖bd1 g5 29 fg ♗xe5 30 ♗f2 d4 ∓∓ 31 ♘h4 ♗b8 32 ♕b6 ♕f4 33 g3 ♕f2+ 34 ♔h1 ♗e2 0-1.

10 ed
Or 10 ♘xc6 bc 11 ed ♘xd5 12 ♘xd5 cd 13 ♗f3 ♗a6 = Carlson-Helmertz, U.S. Open Ch 1978.

10 ... ♘xd5
11 ♘xd5 ♕xd5 12 ♗f3 ♕a5! 13 ♘xc6 bc 14 ♗xc6 ♖b8 15 ♕d5 ♕c7 16 ♗a4 ♗xb2 17 ♖ad1 ♗a6 ∓ Ravinsky-Lisitsin, 13th USSR Ch 1944.

B:

9 f3 d5! (Not 9 ... ♕b6. 10 ♘a4 followed by 11 c4 and a Maroczy bind when White has a good game.) 10 ed ♘xd5 11 ♘xd5 ♕xd5 =.

C:

9 ♔h1 d5
10 ed
After 10 ♘xc6 bc 11 e5 ♘d7 12 f4 e6 followed by ... f6 Black will have undermined White's centre and he then has nothing to fear.

10 ... ♘xd5
More interesting is 10 ... ♘b4 11 d6 ♕xd6 12 ♘db5 ♕b8 13 a4 ♗f5 14 ♘a3 ♖d8 Sampokw - Mascarinas, Wellington 1978.

D:

9 f4 (36)

36
B

This holds up Black's normal central thrust 9 ... d5 because then comes 10 e5! (White does not now need to preface this with the trade of knights which strengthens Black's centre.)

9 ... ♕b6
The inadequacy of White's last move is highlighted. Black threatens to win a pawn by 10 ... ♘xe4 as well as 10 ♕xb2 and he is putting pressure along both the b6-g1 and g7-a1 diagonals. White must be content to hold the balance.

9 ... ♗e6 is obviously not yet feasible.

Quieter development by 9 ... ♗d7 10 ♔h1 (10 ♕d2 is also good.) 10 ... ♖c8 11 ♘b3 a6 12 ♗f3 ♕c7 allows White a spatial advantage by 13 ♘d5 as in Euwe-Landau, Delft 1940.

The attempt to exploit the criss-crossing black diagonals by **9 ... ♘g4?** fails to 10

7 Ninth Move Divergences

♗×g4 ♗×d4 (Not 10 ... ♗×g4 11 ♘×c6 winning a piece) 11 ♗×d4 ♗×g4 12 ♕d2! threatening 13 f5! as in Lasker-Golmayo, match 1893.

We now consider:
D1: 10 ♘f5?
D2: 10 ♕d2?
D3: 10 ♘a4
D4: 10 ♕d3
D5: 10 e5!?

D1:
10 ♘f5? loses to 10 ... ♕×b2 11 ♘a4 ♕a3 12 c3 ♘×e4! 13 ♗c1 ♘×c3 14 ♗×a3 ♘×d1 15 ♘×g7 ♘e3.

D2:
10 ♕d2? loses a pawn after 10 ... ♘×e4! 11 ♘×e4 ♗×d4.

D3:
10 ♘a4 can lead after
a) 10 ... ♕a5 to a repetition of moves by 11 ♘c3 ♕b6 12 ♘a4
b) 10 ... ♕b4 11 c3 ♕a5 12 b4 ♕c7 13 ♗f3 ♗d7 14 ♖c1 (Pospisil-Alster, Czechoslovakia 1949) 14 ... ♖ab8! to a complicated game which is promising for Black.

D4:
10 ♕d3 *(37)*
This is White's simplest course, exchanging into an even ending.

37
B

10 ...   ♘g4
Until very recently it was thought that 10 ... ♕×b2 is a near fatal error because of **11 a3**, and if **11 ... ♕b6 12 ♘e6 ±±**. Now this assessment must be revised following an interesting innovation from a game played in Poland: (11 a3) ♘×**e4** 12 ♘×c6 (12 ♘a4? ♕×d4! 13 ♗×d4 ♗×d4+ 14 ♔h1 ♘f2+ 15 ♖×f2 ♗×f2 ∓) 12 ... ♘×c3 13 ♘×e7+ ♔h8 14 ♗f3 ♖e8 15 ♘×c8 ♖a×c8 16 ♗×a7 d5 17 ♔h1 b6 18 ♖ae1 ♔g8 19 ♕a6 ♘e4?! 20 ♗×e4! de 21 ♖×e4 ♕×c2 22 ♖×e8+ ♖×e8 23 ♗×b6 ♕c6! 24 a4 ♖a8 ½-½ Wach-Oley, Poland 1973.

Better than 11 a3 is **11 ♖ab1 ♕a3 12 ♘×c6 bc 13 ♘d5 ♕×d3 14 ♘×e7+ ♔h8 15 cd** (Thomson-Levy, Scottish Ch 1974) and now Black's safest course is 15 ... ♗g4 with equal chances.

Now White has:
D41: 11 ♘d5
D42: 11 ♗×g4

7 Ninth Move Divergences

D41:
11 ♘d5

This allows Black to sacrifice his queen for three active minor pieces.

11 ... ♗×d4
12 ♘×b6

Or 12 ♗×g4 ♗×e3+ 13 ♕×e3 ♕×b2 14 ♗×c8 ♖a×c8 15 ♖ab1 ♕×a2 16 ♖×b7 e6 when White does not have quite enough for the pawn.

12 ... ♗×e3+
13 ♔h1

Not 13 ♕×e3 ♘×e3 14 ♘×a8 ♘×f1 15 ♗×f1 f5! ∓ de Jong - Rogman, Match 1933.

13 ... ♗×b6
14 ♗×g4 ♗×g4
15 f5

After 15 c3 ♗e6 16 f5 ♘e5 17 ♕g3 ♗c4 Black's pieces are beautifully placed, Poulson-Weil, Munich 1936.

15 ... gf!

15 ... ♗h5! is also good for Black: Horowitz - Reshevsky, New York 1951, continued 16 ♖ae1 ♘e5 17 ♕h3 f6 18 ♕h4 ♗g4!

16 ef ♘e5
17 ♕g3 ♔h8 18 ♕h4 ♗d8 19 ♖ae1 e6 20 f6 ♗f5 ∓ van den Bosch-Landau, Amsterdam 1939. One of the points of Black's queen 'sacrifice' is that the Dragon pawn formation forms an impregnable barrier to the white queen.

D42:
11 ♗×g4 ♗×d4

Naturally not 11 ... ♘×d4 12 ♘d5! ♕c5 13 ♗×c8 when White wins material.

12 ♗×d4 ♕×d4+
13 ♕×d4 ♘×d4
14 ♗×c8 ♖a×c8 15 ♖f2 ♔g7 16 ♖d1 ♖c4 17 ♖fd2 e5 18 ♖f1 f5 = Mestrović-Hartston, Orebrö 1966.

D5:
10 e5!?

This, the Zollner Gambit, leads to slightly obscure complications at the end of which Black has an extra pawn and White some, but not enough, compensation.

10 ... de
11 fe ♘×e5

Not 11 ... ♖d8 12 ef ♗×f6 13 ♖×f6! ef 14 ♘a4 ♖×d4 15 ♘×b6 ♖×d1+ 16 ♖×d1 ab 17 a3! ± - Veresov.

12 ♘f5 *(38)*

Now Black has:
D51: 12 ... ♕d8
D52: 12 ... ♕e6

7 Ninth Move Divergences

D53: 12... ♕×b2!

D51:
If **12... ♕d8** simply 13 ♕×d8 ♖×d8 14 ♘×e7+ ♔f8 (Or 14... ♔h8 15 ♗g5) 15 ♗c5 ± - Alekhine.

D52:
12...   ♕e6
It seems that White can gain the upper hand after this move.
13 ♘×g7 ♔×g7
14 ♕d2
and now:
a) **14... ♘eg4** 15 ♗d4 ♕d7 (Romatti - de Ronde, Buenos Aires 1939) 16 ♗×g4 ♕×g4 17 ♖×f6! ef 18 ♘d5 winning - Alekhine.
b) **14... ♘g8?** 15 ♘b5 ♕d7 16 ♕c3! with a great advantage. Kramer - Euwe, match 1940.
c) **14... ♔g8** 15 ♖ae1 ♘c6 when:
c1) If 16 ♗d3 ♕d7 17 h3 ♘h5 18 ♕f2 ♘g7 19 ♕h4 ♕d8 20 ♘e4 f6, Nezhmetdinov - Pogrebisky, ½-F USSR Ch 1949, Black can cope with all the threats and should realise his extra pawn.
c2) White should continue with 16 ♗f3! ♕d7 17 ♕f2 followed by ♕h4 when Black's defensive resources are rather strained.

D53:
12...   ♕×b2!

13 ♘×e7+ ♔h8
14 ♗d4
Not:
a) **14 ♕d2?** ♗e6! 15 ♖ab1 ♕a3 16 ♖×b7 ♖fd8 17 ♕e1 ♘e4! 18 ♘d1 ♘c4 19 ♗f4 ♕c5+ 20 ♔h1 ♘cd6 ∓ Sanguinetti - Marini, 1954.
b) **14 ♘×c8?** ♕×c3! 15 ♗d4 (Or 15 ♕d4? ♕×c8 16 ♕×e5 ♘h5 followed by... ♗×a1) 15... ♕×c8 16 ♗×e5 ♖d8 17 ♗d4 (On 17 ♖×f6? ♕c5+ 18 ♗d4 ♖×d4 ∓∓) 17... ♘e4 18 ♗×g7+ ♔×g7 19 ♕e1 ♕c5+ 20 ♔h1 ♕×c2 ∓ White has insufficient compensation for two pawns.

14...   ♕b4!
This move represents the start of a sequence which disproves the old Hungarian adage 'It isn't safe to take the b-pawn even when it is safe to do so'.
14... ♘g8 is not so clear: 15 ♘b5! ♕b4 16 ♘d5 ♕a4 17 ♖f4! g5 18 ♖e4 f6 19 ♘×f6! and now:
a) **19... ♘c6?** 20 ♗c3!! ♕a6 21 ♘×h7 ♕b6+ 22 ♔h1 ♖f5 (Or 22... ♔×h7 23 ♗d3 ♗f5 24 ♕h5+ ♗h6 25 ♖e6!!) 23 ♘×g5! ♗×c3 24 ♖h4+ ♔g7 25 ♖h7+ ♔f8 26 ♘×c3 ♖×g5 27 ♗h5! ♖f5 28 ♕g4 followed by ♕g6 winning, Stalingrad - Saratov, telegraph game 1948.
b) **19... ♗×f6** 20 ♖×e5 ♖d8! 21 ♖e4 ♗d4+ 22

♖xd4 ♖xd4 23 ♘xd4 ♗d7 when, instead of 24 ♘f3, as played in Aratovsky-Ilivitsky, RSFSR corres 1948, 24 ♕d2 followed by ♕c3 and ♗f3 would have given White a positional plus.

Also dubious is **14 ... ♘fg4**, threatening to simplify by ... ♘e3. Castro - Rogoff, Graz 1972 continued: 15 ♘ed5 (better 15 ♖b1! ♕a3 16 ♘xc8) 15 ... ♕a3 16 ♘b5 ♕a5 17 h3 ♘h6 18 ♖f6! ♘c6 19 ♗c3 ♕d8, and now White's best continuation is 20 ♖d6! when according to Rogoff the complications should lead to a draw.

15 ♗xe5
Instead:
a) **15 ♘(either)d5** ♘xd5 16 ♘xd5 ♕xd4+ 17 ♕xd4 ♘f3+ wins for Black.
b) **15 ♘xc8** is also inferior because of:
b1) **15 ... ♖d8** 16 ♘b5 ♖axc8 17 c3 ♕e7 18 ♘xa7 ♖xc3! 19 ♕e1 (Or 19 ♘b5 ♘e4 20 ♕a4 ♖cc8 21 ♗b6 ♘c4 22 ♗xc4? ♗xa1 23 ♖xa1 ♕f6 24 ♗d4 ♖xd4 0-1 Samarian - Roele, Munich 1942) 19 ... ♖c2 20 ♗d1 ♖xd4 21 ♗xc2 ♕c5 22 ♔h1 ♘g8 23 ♗b3? ♕xa7 24 ♗xf7 ♘e7! and Black consolidates his position, Palda-Galia, Schlechter Memorial Tourney, Vienna 1947.

b2) **15 ... ♖axc8** 16 ♗xe5 (Or 16 ♖b1 ♕e7 ∓) 16 ... ♖fd8 17 ♗xf6 ♗xf6! and Black has a distinct positional advantage in addition to his extra pawn.

c) **15 ♖xf6** is flashy but unsound. Black wins by 15 ... ♗xf6 16 ♘ed5 ♘f3+! 17 ♗xf3 ♕xd4+ and his material advantage is decisive.

15 ... ♕xe7
16 ♕d4
The only way to maintain any pressure. White loses after both:
a) **16 ♗xf6?** ♗xf6 17 ♘d5 ♕c5+ and
b) **16 ♗d6** ♕e3+ 17 ♔h1 ♕xc3.

16 ... ♘h5
Not 16 ... ♖d8? 17 ♗xf6 ♖xd4 18 ♗xe7 ♖d7 19 ♗f6! winning a piece.
17 ♗xg7+ ♘xg7
18 ♗d3

This deprives Black's bishop of its best square (f5) and is probably stronger than 18 ♘d5 ♕d6 19 ♖ad1 ♗e6 when White's compensation is insufficient.

18 ... ♗e6 *(39)*

This position is rather difficult to assess. White has some attacking chances based on the weak dark squares near Black's king and on the pin of the Black knight. On the other hand, Black is a pawn ahead and his major pieces have many open lines at

7 Ninth Move Divergences

their disposal. All in all, I consider that Black has the better chances, but there has not yet been any practical experience with this possibly crucial variation.

E:

9 ♘b3

The 'normal' position. 9♘b3 is played in order to hold up Black's central break ... d5.

Black has two main plans: either to try to force the thematic break ... d5, or to play on the Q-side with ... ♗e6, ... ♘a5 and ... ♗c4; or ... a5 to weaken White's Q-flank. Now:

E1: 9 ... ♗d7
E2: 9 ... a5!
E3: 9 ... ♗e6!

E1:

9 ... ♗d7

This is too passive. Black must play actively to engage the white pieces, otherwise White can easily set in motion a pawn storm on the K-side: 10 f4 a6 11 g4! and if 11 ... ♔h8 12 g5 ♘g8 13 f5 ♗e5 14 ♕e1.

E2:

9 ... **a5** (40)

Alekhine's move, which he introduced with success in his game with Spielmann at Margate 1938.

10 a4

White must allow his b4 to be weakened in this way, otherwise the further advance of Black's a-pawn is likely to cause his some embarrassment, e.g.:
a) **10 h3?** a4 11 ♘d4 a3 12 b3 ♕a5 13 ♘db5 ♗d7 14 ♕d2 ♘b4 15 ♘d4 ♖fc8 ∓ Miagmasuren-Soos, Varna 1962.
b) **10 a3** a4 (Or 10 ... ♗e6 11 f4 a4 12 f5 gf 13 ef ♗×f5 14 ♖×f5 ab 15 cb ♕d7 16 ♗d3 ♖a5 ∓ Fries - Nielsen - Ristić, Graz 1978.) 11 ♘d4 d5 12 ed ♘×d5 13 ♘×d5 ♕×d5 14 ♗f3 ♕a5 15 ♘×c6 (Or 15 ♗×c6? bc 16 ♘×c6 ♕c7 ∓) 15 ... bc 16 ♗×c6 ♖a6 ∓ Berkov-Goldberg, USSR 1939.

c) The slow evasive **10 ♘d2** is easily handled: 10... ♗e6 11 ♘c4 b5 12 ♘×b5 ♘×e4 13 ♘d4 ♘×d4 14 ♗×d4 ♖b8 15 ♗×g7 ♔×g7 16 ♕d4+ ♘f6 17 ♖ad1 ♕c7 18 b3 ♖fc8 ∓ Kopayev - Averbakh, USSR 1952.

10... ♗e6

10... ♘b4 should be met by 11 f4 when:

a) **11 ... ♗e6** produces a position similar to many in variation A1, chapter 9, p.69, but with the important difference that here Black's queen is on d8 instead of c8 and therefore after 12 f5 the reply 12... ♗c4 is impossible.

b) **11 ... ♗d7** 12 ♗f3 ♕c8 13 h3 ♗e6 (what else?) and Black is a tempo behind variation D3, p.75; Janosević - Fuderer, Yugoslavia 1951, continued 14 ♘d4 ♗c4 15 ♖f2 ♖d8 16 ♖d2 ♘d7 and now 17 ♘db5 would have given White the advantage.

Now White has:
E21: 11 f4
E22: 11 ♘d4

E21:

11 f4 ♖c8

11... ♕c8 transposing into Tartakower's line (variation A1, chapter 9, p.69) is Black's most solid line.

On **11 ... ♘d7** there can follow:

a) 12 f5? ♗×b3 13 cb ♘c5 14 ♗c4 ♘e5 15 ♗d5 ♖c8 when Black has the initiative. Denes - Troianescu, Bucharest 1960.

b) **12 ♕d2** ♗×b3 13 cb ♘c5 14 ♗×c5 dc 15 ♕×d8 ♖a×d8 = Beni - Trifunović, Helsinki 1952.

c) **12 ♗f3** ♘b4 transposing into Bronstein-Korchnoi, Leningrad 1959. (See chapter 3, variation B, p.22.)

12 f5 ♗×b3

Or 12 ... ♗d7 13 g4 ♘e5 14 ♘d2 ♗c6 15 g5 ♘fd7 16 ♕e1 f6 17 h4 ♘c5 18 ♕g3 ± Nei-Ragozin, USSR 1952.

13 cb ♘b4

Despite the central pawn majority and good squares at e5 and b4 Black has very little creative play and the two bishops give White some advantage.

14 ♗c4! ♘d7

Not 14... ♘×e4 15 fg hg 16 ♖×f7! ♖×f7 17 ♗×f7+ ♔×f7 18 ♘×e4, when Black has many weaknesses.

15 ♕e2!

This is stronger than 15 ♘d5 ♘×d5 16 ♗×d5 ♘f6 17 ♗×b7 ♖b8 18 ♗c6 ♖b4! ∓ Janosević - Averbakh, Titovo Uzice 1966.

15 ... ♘e5

Liberzon - Pavlenko, USSR Armed Forces Ch 1968 continued: 16 ♗b5! ♘a6 17 ♘d5

7 Ninth Move Divergences

♘c5 18 ♗g5 f6 19 ♗e3 g5 20 ♖a3, and the light-square weaknesses in Black's position ensured White an advantage.

E22:
11 ♘d4   d5!

Alekhine's continuation. Also possible is 11 ... ♘×d4 12 ♗×d4 and now:

a) **12 ... ♕c7** 13 ♖e1 ♖ac8 14 ♗d3 ♗c4 15 e5 de 16 ♗×e5 ♕c6 17 ♗×c4 ♕×c4 18 ♕f3 ♕b4 19 h3 ♖fd8 20 ♕e2 e6 21 ♖a3 ♘d5 (Tolush-Kitayev, corres 1967) 22 ♗×g7! ±

b) **12 ... ♖c8** 13 f4 ♗c4 14 ♖f2 e5 when, for the offered pawn, Black obtains active play, Tolush-Rovner, Leningrad Ch 1939.

c) **12 ... ♘d7** is recommended by Gufeld and Lazarev.

Exchanging knights in the centre is too simplifying and does not give White enough opportunity to go wrong. 11 ... d5! only leads to equality, it is true, but it does set White a few problems on the way.

12 ♘×e6
12 ed ♗×d5 13 ♘×d5 ♘×d5 14 ♘×c6 bc was played in Spielmann-Alekhine, Margate 1938, which continued 15 ♗d4 e5 16 ♗c5 ♖e8 17 ♗c4 ♕c7 18 c3 (Not 18 ♗×d5 cd 19 ♕×d5 ♖ad8 20 ♕c4 ♖c8) 18 ... ♖ad8 19

♕c2 e4! (simultaneously increasing Black's space, vacating the useful e5 square and preventing b4.) 20 ♖ad1 ♕e5 21 ♖fe1 ♕h5! (By attacking the rook at d1 Black indirectly defends the advanced e-pawn and keeps his queen actively placed.) 22 ♕e2 ♕×e2 23 ♖×e2 ♖b8 24 ♗a3 ♗f8 25 ♗×f8 ♔×f8 26 ♖ed2 ½-½.

12 ...   fe
13 ed   ♘×d5!

Not 13 ... ed? 14 ♘b5 e5 15 c3, e.g.:

a) **15 ... ♔h8** 16 ♕b3 ± Horowitz-Reshevsky, New York 1941.

b) **15 ... ♕e7** 16 ♕b3 ♔h8 17 ♖ad1 ♖ad8 18 ♗b6 ± Franke-Meyer, corres 1959.

c) **15 ... ♖f7** 16 ♕b3 ♖d7 17 f4 ♕e7 18 ♖ae1 e4? 19 g4 ♕e6 20 f5 gf 21 gf with attacking chances for White, Wason-Castaldi, corres.

But instead of 14 ... e5 Black can try the new move **14 ... e6**, as in Hallberg - Sundstedt, Sweden 1978: 15 c3 ♖f7 with roughly equal chances.

14 ♗d2!

After this straightforward move, in the opinion of Gufeld and Lazarev, Black has insufficient compensation for his pawn weaknesses.

If 14 ♗g4 ♘×e3 15 ♗×e6+ ♔h8 16 fe ♕b6 ∓ -

Boleslavsky.

E3:
9 ... ♗e6! *(41)*

41 W

The main line.

Despite the fact that 9 ... a5 gives good chances of equalising, the text has been the reply almost invariably seen from the normal position. The reason for this is that those who play the Dragon usually do so because it produces lively games in which the tactics very often go in Black's favour. 9 ... ♗e6 keeps more pieces on the board than 9 ... a5 (and its exchanging sequence starting with 11 ... d5!), and hence it gives White, if he is not well-versed in Dragon theory, more opportunity to flounder in the complications.

The purpose of 9 ... ♗e6 is threefold:
a) It prepares the centre break ... d5.
b) It gives Black the option of using his c4 square through ... ♘a5 followed by ... ♗c4

or ... ♘c4;
c) It prepares ... ♕c8 (threatening ♘g4/♗g4) followed by either ... ♖d8 (playing for ... d5) or ... a5 with play on the Q-wing.

Now White has:
E31: 10 h3
E32: 10 f3
E33: 10 f4!

E31:
10 h3 d5 11 ed ♘×d5 12 ♘×d5 ♕×d5 13 ♕×d5 ♗×d5 =

E32:
10 f3 d5 11 ed ♘×d5 12 ♘×d5 ♕×d5 13 ♕×d5 ♗×d5 =

E33:
10 f4!

This is the only reasonable way to hold up the equalising ... d5.

Black now has two satisfactory moves:
10 ... ♘a5 which is covered in chapter 8, starting on p. 60.
10 ... ♕c8 which is dealt with in chapter 9, starting on p. 69.

Alternatives are:
a) 10 ... d5? 11 f5! and now:
a1) 11 ... ♗c8 12 ed ♘b4 13 fg hg 14 ♗f3 ♗f5 15 ♘d4 ♘b×d5 16 ♘×d5 ♘×d5 17 ♗×d5 ♕×d5 18 ♘×f5 wins.
a2) 11 ... gf 12 ef ♗c8 13 g4 with a great advantage.

b) 10 ... ♛d7? 11 ♛e1 ±
c) 10 ... ♖c8 has now completely disappeared from master praxis; Rauzer-Chekhover, 8th USSR Ch 1933, went 11 h3 a6 12 ♛d2 b5 13 ♗f3 ♘d7! 14 ♛f2 ♘a5 15 g4? ♘c4! 16 f5 ♘xb2!? (16 ... ♘xe3!).
d) 10 ... b5!? 11 f5 b4? (11 ... ♗xb3 12 ab b4 ±) 12 fe bc 13 ef+ ♔h8 14 bc ♘e5 15 ♗d4 ± Spassky-Miles, Bugojno 1978.

8 Maroczy's 10 ... ♘a5

1 e4 c5 2 ♘f3 d6 3 d4 cd 4 ♘×d4 ♘f6 5 ♘c3 g6 6 ♗e2 ♗g7 7 ♗e3 ♘c6 8 0-0 0-0 9 ♘b3 ♗e6 10 f4
    10 ...   ♘a5 *(42)*

42
W

This move, initiating Q-side counterplay based on either ... ♘c4 or ... ♗c4, was first played in the game Marco - Maroczy, Monte Carlo 1903.

After 10 ... ♘a5 White has
A: 11 e5
B: 11 ♗d4
C: 11 ♘×a5
D: 11 ♘d4
E: 11 g4
F: 11 f5

The most usual move has been 11 f5. The other alternatives, however plausible, should give White no joy.

A:
    11 e5 ♘e8 12 ♘d5 ♘×b3 (12 ... ♘c6 13 ed ♕×d6 14 c4 ±) 13 ab de 14 ♗f3 ef 15 ♘×f4, and now 15 ... ♘d6 consolidates Black's extra pawn. (Hotchkiss-Dimock, postal game 1934, went: 15 ... ♕×d1? 16 ♖f×d1 ♗f5 17 ♘d5 ±)

B:
    11 ♗d4 ♖c8 12 ♗×a7 ♖×c3! 13 bc ♘×e4 14 ♗d4 ♘×c3 15 ♗×c3 ♗×c3 16 ♖b1 ♘c6, and Black's active pieces give him excellent play for the sacrificed material. Rabinovich & Ilyin-Zhenevsky - Levenfish & Ragozin, Leningrad 1933.

C:
    11 ♘×a5 ♕×a5
    12 ♗f3
    12 ♕d2 produces a level position, e.g. 12 ... ♖ac8 13 ♖ad1 (13 ♘d5? ♕×d2 14 ♘×e7+ ♔h8 15 ♗×d2

8 *Maroczy's 10 ... ♘a5*

R×c2) 13 ... Rfe8 14 Bf3 (14 Bd4 Bc4) 14 ... Rc4 15 Qe2 Rec8 =/∓ Guimares-Klauser, Switzerland 1977-8.

12 ... Bc4
13 Re1

If 13 Rf2 Rfd8 14 Qd2 Qc7 15 b3 Ba6 16 Rd1 Rac8 17 ♘d5 ♘×d5 18 ed Bc3! ∓ Treybal-Foltys, Czechoslovakia 1940.

13 ... Rfd8
14 Qd2 Qc7
15 Rac1

More active is 15 Qf2.

15 ... e5!
16 fe

Not 16 b3? d5! e.g.:

a) **17 ed** e4! 18 bc ef 19 c5 Qa5 20 Red1 (20 Qd3! b6!) 20 ... ♘g4! 21 Bd4 f2+ 22 Kf1 (22 Kh1 R×d5! 23 ♘×d5 f1=Q+) 22 ... Qa6+ 23 Qe2 B×d4! 24 R×d4 Qf6 25 Rcd1 Qh4 26 Qd3 Re8 27 Re4 f5 28 Re6 ♘×h2+ 29 Ke2 Q×f4 0-1, Rauzer-Botvinnik, 8th USSR Ch 1933.

b) **17 fe** ♘×e4 18 B×e4 de 19 Qf2 B×e5 20 ♘×e4 f5 ∓

c) **17** ♘×**d5** B×d5 18 ed e4! 19 Be2 ♘×d5 ∓

16 ... de
17 Qf2 b6
18 g4 h6 =

D:

11 ♘d4 Bc4 12 Bd3 Rc8 13 Qf3 (Yudovich - Ragozin, Moscow-Leningrad 1933) 13 ... e5 14 ♘de2 d5!? 15 fe ♘d7 ∓.

E:

11 g4 Bc4

Not 11 ... ♘c4? 12 Bd4! Rc8 (if 12 ... ♘×b2 13 Qc1 ♘c4 14 f5 with a winning attack) 13 f5 Bd7 14 g5 ♘e8 15 B×g7 ♘×g7 (if 15 ... K×g7 16 f6+! ef 17 gf+ ♘×f6 18 Qd4 ♘e5 19 Q×d6 ±) 16 f6! ef 17 gf ♘e8 18 ♘d5 with a big plus. Geszosz-Pribyl, Decin 1973.

12 Bd3 ♘×b3
Better is 12 ... e5 13 g5 ♘h5

13 ab B×d3
14 cd h5 15 h3 d5 16 Ra4! de 17 de hg 18 e5 ♘h7 19 hg g5 20 Rd4 Qb6 21 ♘d5 Qe6 22 ♘c7 with a clear advantage. Mangini-Rojahn, Helsinki 1952.

F:

11 f5

This move gives White the best attacking chances.

11 ... Bc4

Alternatives are clearly out of the question, e.g.:

a) **11 ... gf?** 12 ef Bc4 13 g4 just helps White's attack.

b) **11 ... Bd7** 12 e5! de 13 fg hg (13 ... ♘×b3 14 gh+ ±) 14 ♘×a5 Q×a5 15 R×f6

±±
After 11 ... ♗c4 White has the following alternatives:
F1: 12 fg
F2: 12 g4
F3: 12 ♘×a5
F4: 12 ♗d3
F5: 12 ♔h1

F1:

12 fg leads to equality after 12 ... hg 13 e5 ♗×e2 14 ♕×e2 de 15 ♕b5 ♘×b3 16 ab b6.

F2:

12 g4

This dangerous-looking move was first introduced in Milner-Barry - Foltys, Buenos Aires Olympiad 1939.
12 ...   ♖c8!
After **12 ... ♘d7?** White can transpose into variation F35 by 13 ♘×a5 ♗×e2 14 ♕×e2 ♕×a5 15 ♘d5. **12 ... ♗×e2** 13 ♕×e2 ♘d7 14 ♘×a5 ♕×a5 15 ♘d5 is inferior for Black.
13 ♗×a7!
This is best.
After 13 e5 there can come:
a) **13 ... ♗×e2** 14 ♕×e2 de 15 ♖ad1 ♕c7 16 g5 ♘h5 17 ♘d5 ♕c4, Aitken-Winter, London 1950, and now 18 ♕g2! would have been very strong, e.g. 18 ... ♘c6 19 f6 ef 20 gf ♗h8 21 ♘a5! ±±.

b) **13 ... de!** 14 ♕×d8 ♖f×d8 15 ♘×a5 ♗×e2 16 ♘×e2 ♖×c2 17 ♖fd1 Aitken-Footner, British Ch Whitby 1962, and now 17 ... ♖×d1+ 18 ♖×d1 ♘×g4 leaves White without a satisfactory line, e.g. 19 ♖d8+ ♗f8 20 f6 ef 21 ♗×a7 ♔g7 22 h3 ♖×e2 23 hg ♖×b2 and Black's pawn mass is overwhelming - Golombek.
13 ...   ♗×e2
14 ♕×e2 ♘c4 =

F3:

12 ♘×a5   ♗×e2
13 ♕×e2
Or 13 ♘×b7 ♗×d1 14 ♘×d8 ♗×c2 15 ♘c6 ♖fe8 16 fg hg = Lasker-Riumin, Moscow 1936.
13 ...   ♕a5
14 g4 *(43)*

Initiating the Stockholm Attack which was introduced by the English team (influenced by P.S.Milner-Barry) at the Stockholm Olympiad 1937. This is a crucial position for Dragon

8 Maroczy's 10 ... ♘a5

theory, and the multiplicity of moves at Black's disposal has been the subject of much controversy.

We examine:
F31: 14 ... ♕e5
F32: 14 ... d5?
F33: 14 ... h6
F34: 14 ... ♕b4?
F35: 14 ... ♘d7?
F36: 14 ... ♖ac8!

The popularity of the Stockholm Attack was so prevalent during a period that spanned three decades that just about every reasonable move has been tried from the crucial position shown in diagram 43. 14 ... ♖ac8! together with the exchange sacrifice that it prepares is the only way for Black to avoid getting the inferior game.

F31:
14 ... ♕e5 15 ♕f3 d5 16 ♘×d5 (16 ed? ♘×g4 17 ♕×g4 ♕×e3+ winning) 16 ... ♘×d5 17 ed ± Estrin-Alexeyev, Leningrad 1948.

F32:
14 ... d5? 15 e5 ♘d7 16 ♗d4 ♖fe8 17 ♖ae1 e6 18 f6 ± Kulis-Aim, 1944.

F33:
14 ... h6
15 ♔h1! ♖ac8
15 ... g5? 16 h4! or 15 ...

♕b4 16 a3 ♕×b2 17 ♗d4! and 18 ♖a2 ±
16 g5   hg
17 ♗×g5

and now:
a) **17** ... ♕b4 18 ♖ab1 ♖×c3 19 bc ♕×e4+ 20 ♕×e4 ♘×e4 21 ♗×e7 ♖c8 22 f6 ♗h6 23 ♖×b7 ±
b) **17** ... ♖fe8 18 ♕g2! ♘h7 19 fg fg (19 ... ♘×g5 20 gf+ ♘×f7 21 ♖f5! ♕b4 22 ♖g1 ♕d4 23 e5! ±±) 20 ♘d5 ± Rabinovich - Lisitsin, Leningrad 1940.

F34:
14 ... ♕b4? (44)

44
W

15 g5

White can play for an advantage with 15 ♖ad1 ♖fe8 16 ♗d4 ♘d7 17 ♗×g7 ♔×g7 18 ♕f3 f6 19 g5 ± but the text is even stronger.

Black now has:
F341: 15 ... ♘×e4?
F342: 15 ... ♘h5
F343: 15 ... ♘d7

F341:

Not 15 ... ♘×e4? 16 ♘d5 ♕×b2 17 ♘×e7+ ♔h8 18 f6 ±±

F342:
15 ...   ♘h5

This has been found to be faulty.

16 a3   ♕×b2
17 ♘d5   ♖ae8

On 17 ... ♕e5 18 ♕d3 ♘g3 19 c3! is very strong as White threatens 20 ♗d4, and Black cannot play 19 ... ♕×e4 because of 20 ♕×e4 ♘×e4 21 ♘×e7+ ♔h8 22 f6!

18 ♕f2!   ♕e5

Not 18 ... ♕×a1 19 ♖×a1 ♗×a1 20 c3!

19 f6   ef
20 gf   ♗h8
21 ♖ae1!   ♖e6 22 ♗d4 ♕g5+ 23 ♔h1 ♖fe8 24 ♖g1 ♕h6 25 ♕h4 ± Estrin - Fridstein, Moscow 1945.

F343:
15 ...   ♘d7
16 a3

16 ♗d2 is also good for White.

16 ...   ♕×b2

Or 16 ... ♕a5 17 ♘d5 ♕d8 18 ♕f2 ♗×b2 19 ♖ab1 ♗e5 20 f6 ±

17 ♘d5   ♖ae8

The alternatives are no better. Rabinovich analysed:

a) 17 ... e6 18 ♘e7+ ♔h8 19 f6 ♘×f6 20 gf ♗×f6 21 ♕f2! winning (21 ... ♗×e7 22 ♗d4+)

b) 17 ... ♕×a1 18 ♖×a1 ♗×a1 19 c3 e6 20 ♘e7+ ♔h8 21 ♕d2 and White, who is threatening both 23 ♕×d6 and 23 ♕c1 winning the bishop, has an easily won game — Rabinovich.

18 ♖ab1!

18 ♖ad1 only leads to a draw after 18 ... ♗e5 19 ♗c1 ♕a1 20 ♖f3 ♘c5 21 ♗f4 ♕b2 22 ♗c1 ♕a1 etc., but 18 ♕f2 is an interesting and strong-looking alternative which has never been tested.

18 ...   ♕e5

Or 18 ... ♕×a3 19 ♖×b7! ±±

19 ♖b4

Threatening to win the queen by 20 ♗f4

19 ...   gf
20 ♗f4   ♕e6
21 ♘c7   ♕g6 22 ♘×e8 ♖×e8 23 ♕b5 ♖d8 24 ef ♔h5 25 f6! ef 26 gf ♕×b5 27 ♖×b5 ♗×f6 28 ♖×b7. White has a winning advantage.

F35:
14 ...   ♘d7? *(45)*

This used to be considered Black's best antidote to the Stockholm Attack, but after a time it became apparent that Black's difficulties are still considerable.

15 ♘d5   ♖ae8

8 Maroczy's 10 ... ♘a5   65

45
W

After 15 ... e6 16 ♘e7+ ♔h8, Black is given no time to set about winning the lonely-looking knight: 17 g5 ef (17 ... ♖fe8 18 f6 ♗f8 19 ♖ad1 ±±) 18 ef ♗xb2 19 ♖ab1 ♕e5 20 ♖xb2! ♕xb2 21 ♖d1 ♘e5 22 ♗d4 ♕b4 23 fg! ±, Ilyin - Zhenevsky - Volk, Leningrad 1940.
16 g5!
Much stronger than **16 b4** ♕d8 17 ♖ad1 e6! 18 fg fg 19 ♖xf8+ ♘xf8 20 ♘f4= - Ragozin.

Also of dubious value is **16 ♗g5** ♕c5+ 17 ♔h1 ♘f6 18 ♗e3 ♕c6 19 ♕g2 ♘xd5 20 ed ♕a6 21 c3 ♖c8 22 ♖f3 b5 ∓ Bellon-Oltra, Benidorm 1978.

16 ...   e6
17 ♘e7+   ♖xe7
18 f6   ♖ee8
19 fg   ♔xg7
20 ♖ad1

For the sacrificed pawn, White has more than enough compensation in the form of pressure on the queen's pawn and the possibility of an attack along the long diagonal - Sokolsky.

F36:
14 ...   ♖ac8! *(46)*

46
W

Originally thought to be an error, but thanks to an exchange sacrifice suggested by Simagin, we now know that this is the only line which is satisfactory (even good) for Black.
15 g5
Boleslavsky demonstrates that 15 ♗d4 also allows Black good play. His analysis runs: 15 ... ♕b4 16 ♖ad1 ♕c4 17 ♖d3 ♘d7 18 ♗xg7 ♔xg7 19 ♕d2 ♘f6 20 ♖h3 g5! (20 ... ♘xg4 21 ♖f4!) 21 ♕xg5+ ♔h8 22 ♕h6 ♖g8 23 g5 ♖xg5+ 24 ♕xg5 ♖g8 and on the open board Black's queen is more powerful than White's rooks.
15 ...   ♖xc3!
The move that refutes the Stockholm Attack! Before Simagin's suggestion was known to the world, everyone assumed

15 ... ♘d7 to be essential when 16 ♘d5! would give White a strong bind.
16 gf
16 bc ♘×e4 would clearly be advantageous to Black.
16 ... ♖×e3
17 ♕×e3 ♗×f6
18 c3 ♖c8

Simagin ends his analysis here with the opinion that Black's counterplay should be sufficient compensation for the exchange. Practical experience bears out his assessment.

19 a3

Attacking on the king-side fails to reap White any dividends because his own king becomes too exposed. Davie-Whiteley, Brecon 1962 went: 19 ♖f3 b5 20 ♔h1 ♖c4 21 ♖h3 ♗g7 ∓.

19 ... ♖c4

19 ... a6 is also good, freeing the queen from the defence of this pawn. Pavlov-Mititelu, Bucharest 1962 continued: 20 ♖ae1 ♕b5 21 ♖e2 ♔g7 22 ♖f3 h6 23 ♖h3 g5 24 ♕d3 ♕c5+ 25 ♕e3 ♕c4 ∓.

20 ♖ae1 b5!

The best way for Black to minimise the effect of White's slight material advantage is to launch a minority attack on the Q-side.

21 ♖f3 ♕c7
22 fg hg

23 ♖h3 a5!

Now White has no means of preventing an eventual ... b4, and with it the isolating of yet another of his pawns.

24 ♖f1 ♕c5

White was threatening 25 ♖×f6! ef 26 ♕h6

25 ♕×c5 ♖×c5
26 ♖d3 ♖c4
27 ♖×f6

If 27 ♖e1 b4 28 ab ab 29 cb ♗×b2 30 ♖b3 ♗c3! 31 ♖eb1 ♗d4+ 32 ♔h1 (Otherwise 32 ... ♖c2 is very strong) 32 ... ♗b6 33 ♖e1 ♔g7! and White will find it difficult to hang on to all his isolated pawns.

27 ... ef
28 ♖×d6 ♖×e4
29 ♖×f6 ♔g7 30 ♖b6 ♖e5 31 ♔f2 g5 32 ♖a6 a4 33 c4 ♖c5 34 cb ♖×b5 35 ♖×a4 ♖×b2+ 36 ♔g3 ½-½, Filipowicz-Hollis, Marianske Lazne 1962.

F4:

12 ♗d3 *(47)*

47
B

8 Maroczy's 10 ... ♘a5

Spielmann's move, holding the centre intact and preparing for a K-side attack with g4-g5 etc.

12 ...   ♗×d3

Trying to keep some sort of tension in the position is often the best plan for Black in the Dragon, but here the only methods of doing so are to Black's detriment, viz:

a) **12 ... b5?** 13 ♘×b5 (Or 13 ♘×a5 ♕×a5 14 ♗×c4 bc 15 ♗d3 ♖ab8 16 ♖b1 ♖b7 17 g4 ♘d7 18 ♘d5 ♗×d4 19 ♕×d4 ♘b6 20 ♘e3 ± Petrushin-Perespkin, 1st L 45th USSR Ch 1977) 13 ... ♗×b5 14 ♗×b5 ♘×e4 15 ♘×a5 ♕×a5 16 ♗c6 ±±.

b) **12 ... d5?** 13 e5 and now:

b1) **13 ... ♘e8** 14 ♘×a5 ♕×a5 15 ♗d4 ±, though the recent game Parma-Rajkovic, Yugoslav Ch 1978 may cast doubt on this assessment: 15 ... ♖d8 16 ♔h1 ♕a6 17 ♗c5 ♗×d3 18 cd ♖d7 19 f6 ef 20 ♗×f8 ♔×f8 21 ef ♘×f6 22 ♕f3 h5 ∞

b2) **13 ... ♘×b3** 14 ef ♗×f6 15 ab ♗×d3 16 ♕×d3 d4 17 fg dc 18 gf+ ♖×f7 19 bc ± Kashdan - Denker, New York 1941.

b3) **13 ... ♗×d3** 14 ef ♗×f1 15 fg ♔×g7 16 ♕d4+ f6 17 ♖×f1 ±±

13 cd

13 ♕×d3 ♘×b3 14 ab

♘g4 gives Black a minimal advantage because of his control of e5.

Now Black has:

F41: 13 ... ♘×b3
F42: 13 ... ♘c6
F43: 13 ... d5

F41:

13 ...   ♘×b3
14 ab

Or 14 ♕×b3 ♘g4!

14 ...   d5
15 ♗d4!   de
16 de   a6

Not 16 ... ♕c7 (16 ... ♘d7 17 ♘d5!) 17 e5 ♖ad8 18 ef ♗×f6 19 ♖a4! b5 20 ♘×b5 ♕d7 21 ♕e2 a6 22 ♗×f6! ab 23 ♗×e7 ba 24 ♗×f8 ♔×f8 25 ba and White's outside passed pawn will decide the issue - Spielmann.

17 e5   ♘e8

If:

a) **17 ... ♘d5** 18 ♕g4 threatens ♖f3-h3 followed by ♕h4; and 18 ... ♘b4? fails against 19 f6 ef 20 ef ♗h6 21 ♗c5.

b) **17 ... ♘d7** White gets a good game by 18 ♕e2 ♘b8 19 ♖ad1 ♘c6 20 ♗c5 ♕a5 21 b4! ♘×b4 22 ♗×e7 etc.

18 ♕g4!

The suggestion of Boleslavsky gives White the advantage because of his superior mobility and extra space on the K-side.

F42:

13 ... ♘c6 gives White too much freedom in the centre, viz: 14 d4 b5 15 ♕f3 b4 16 ♘e2 ♕c7 17 g4 a5 18 ♖ad1 a4 19 ♘bc1 ♖ac8 20 ♘d3 ♕b7 21 g5 ♘d7 22 ♘df4 ± Goldberg-Kotlerman, ½F 19th USSR Ch 1951.

F43:
    13 ...   d5
    15 ♘×a5

Not 14 e5? (14 ♗d4? ♘c6 15 ♗×f6 ♗×f6 16 ♘×d5 ♗×b2 ∓) 14 ... ♘×b3 15 ef ♗×f6 16 ♕×b3 d4 17 ♗h6 dc 18 ♗×f8 cb 19 ♖ab1 ♕d4+ ∓

    14 ...   ♕×a5
    15 e5

Again ♗d4 is inappropriate. After 15 ... de 16 de ♖fd8 Black has the initiative.

    15 ...   d4!
    16 ♗×d4

Aitken's 16 ef ♗×f6 17 fg dc (not 17 ... hg? 18 ♖ f6) 18 gh+ can be met by 18 ... ♔h8 (not 18 ... ♔×h7 19 ♖f3); White's advanced h-pawn will not run away and until he is ready to capture it Black can use it as a shield. Meanwhile White is forced into the continuation: 19 bc ♕×c3 when both his Q-side pawns are isolated and the d-pawn is particularly vulnerable on the semi-open file.

    16 ...   ♘d7
    17 f6   ef
    18 ef   ♗×f6

Not 18 ... ♘×f6?? 19 ♗×f6 ♕b6+ 20 ♔h1 ♗×f6 21 ♘d5 and White wins.

    19 ♖×f6!?

If 19 ♗×f6 ♕b6+ =.

The text is a new attempt at refuting 10 ... ♘a5.

    19 ...   ♘×f6
    20 ♕f3   ♘d7
    21 ♕×b7
    21 ♘d5 ♖ae8 ∓.
    21 ...   ♖ad8
    22 ♘d5   ♖fe8
    23 b4   ♕a4

And not 23 ... ♕a3? 24 ♗c3 ± Rantanen - Helmers, Kringsja 1978.

9 Tartakower's 10 ... ♕c8

1 e4 c5 2 ♘f3 d6 3 d4 cd 4 ♘×d4 ♘f6 5 ♘c3 g6 6 ♗e2 ♗g7 7 ♗e3 ♘c6 8 0-0 0-0 9 ♘b3 ♗e6 10 f4
10 ...   ♕c8 *(48)*

48
W

This was played in Réti - Tartakower, New York 1924. In the tournament book Alekhine wrote 'Black's entire structure makes an artificial impression'. For the further moves see 11 h3 ♘e8?

Black's 10 ... ♕c8, besides holding up White's f5, can be a preparation for 'freeing' exchanges on Black's g4 or c4.

After 10 ... ♕c8 White has:
A: 11 ♔h1
B: 11 ♕d2
C: 11 ♕e1
D: 11 h3

A:

11 ♔h1
Now Black has:
A1: 11 ... a5
A2: 11 ... ♖d8

If **11** ... ♘g4, 12 ♗g1 is good for White, as is **11** ... ♗g4 12 ♗g1 b6 13 ♘d5 (Stronger than 13 ♘d4 ♗×e2 14 ♕×e2 ♕b7 15 ♖ad1 ♖ac8 16 ♘d5 ♖fe8 17 c4 ♘×d5 18 ed ♘×d4 19 ♗×d4 e5 20 de ♖×e6 ∓ Hase-Sosonko, Buenos Aires OL 1978) 13 ... ♗×e2 14 ♕×e2 ♕b7 15 ♖ad1 ♖fe8 16 c3 ♖ac8 17 ♗f2 ♘b8 18 ♕f3 ♕a6 19 ♘×f6+ ♗×f6 20 e5! Savon - Sosonko, Ljubljana/Portoroz 1977.

A1:

11 ...   a5
12 ♘d4!
On 12 a4 Black can play **12** ... ♘b4! with a satisfactory game. Also possible is **12** ... ♗g4 13 ♗g1 (13 ♗×g4

♘×g4 14 ♗g1 ♘b4 = Cholasuran - Mednis, Varna 1962, is a quiet line.) 13 ... ♖e8! (better than 13 ... ♖d8 14 ♘d5! ♗×e2 15 ♕×e2 ♘×d5 16 ed ± Alekhine - Golombek, Montevideo 1939) and if 14 ♘d5 ♗×e2 15 ♕×e2 ♘×d5 16 ed ♘b4 17 c4 e6! with adequate play - Kan.
    12 ... ♘×d4
    13 ♗×d4 ♗c4
    14 ♗d3! ±
The typical counter 14 ... e5, available with the white king at g1, is ineffective here as the black queen has no check at c5 (compare variation D36, p. 77, note to White's 16th move).

A2:
    11 ...   **♖d8**
    12 ♗g1! *(49)*

Bronstein's improvement on 12 ♗f3 ♗c4 (If **12 ... d5** 13 e5 ♘e4 14 ♘e2 f6 ±. Or **12 ... ♗g4?!** 13 h3 ♗×h3 14 f5 gf 15 gh fe - *15 ... f4? 16 ♗×f4 ♕×h3+ 17 ♔g1 followed by ♗g2 ±* - 16 ♗g2 d5! 17 ♗g5! d4 - *Beni-Busek, 1953* - 18 ♘e2 ±) 13 ♖e1 (On 13 ♖f2 Black can equalise with 13 ... e5!, e.g. **14 ♕d2** - *Ragozin-Aronin, 16th USSR Ch 1948* - 14 ... d5; or **14 ♖d2** ef 15 ♗×f4 ♘e5 16 ♘e2 - *16 ♖×d6 ♖×d6 17 ♕×d6 ♘×f3 18 gf ♘h5 with threats,*

Rossetto-Panno, Portoroz 1958 - 16 ... ♗a6 = Matanović-Geller, Belgrade 1957; or **14 h3** d5 15 ed e4 16 ♗e2 ♘×d5 17 ♘×d5 ♖×d5 18 ♕c1 ♗×e2 19 ♖×e2 b6 ∓ Ryabchenok - Tyulin, Volgograd 1977.) 13 ... e5! 14 ♕d2 ♕c7 15 ♖ad1 ♖ac8 16 ♕f2 b5 17 fe de 18 ♗g5 ♖×d1 19 ♖×d1 ♖d8 20 ♘d5 ½-½, Holmov-Aronin, 17th USSR Ch 1949.

49
B

    12 ...   b6
12 ... d5 13 e5 d4 (13 ... ♘e4 14 ♘b5 ±) 14 ♘b5 ± - Bronstein.

12 ... ♘d7 13 f5 ♗×b3 14 ab ♘b4 15 ♖a4 a5 16 ♘d5 ♘×d5 17 ed ± Rantanen - Osterman, Finnish Ch 1978.
    13 ♕e1   ♘b4
    14 ♖c1   ♗c4
    15 ♗×c4   ♕×c4
    16 ♘d2   ♕c8
    17 a3   ♘c6
    18 ♘f3   ♖b8
Possibly 18 ... e6 is slightly better.
    19 ♘d5   e6

20 ♘xf6+ ♗xf6
21 c3   ♖b7
22 ♗f2! ±
Bronstein - Korchnoi, Hastings 1975-6.

This game has put 10 ... ♕c8 under a cloud for the time being.

B:

11 ♕d2   ♖d8

Or 11 ... a5 12 a4 ♘b4 13 ♘d4 ♗c4 14 f5?! ♘d7! 15 ♗xc4 ♕xc4 16 b3 ♕c5 Dely - Velimirović, Belgrade 1968.
12 ♗f3   ♗c4
13 ♖fd1! e5!
14 ♘d5 ♗xd5 15 ed ♘e7 16 fe de 17 d6 ♘f5 18 ♗c5 e4 19 ♗e2 (Dubinin - Aronin, RSFSR Ch 1947) 19 ... b6! 20 ♗a3 ♘h6 and now 21 ♕e1 ♕e6! ∓; or 21 ♕b4 ♗f8 ∓

C:

11 ♕e1

An interesting alternative intending to reinforce the traditional king's side attack by playing ♕h4. Now Black has:
C1: 11 ... ♘g4
C2: 11 ... ♗g4
C3: 11 ... ♘b4
C4: 11 ... a5!

C1:

11 ...   ♘g4

For a long time this was the accepted refutation of 11 ♕e1.
12 ♗xg4 ♗xg4
13 f5   gf
14 h3   ♗xh3
Not 14 ... f4? 15 ♖xf4 ♗h5 16 ♘d5! ♕d7 17 ♕h4 ♗g6 18 ♖af1 ♖ac8 19 c3 ± Ragozin - Veresov, Moscow 1947.
15 gh   fe
16 ♕h4   f5
17 ♔h1!

This busts the accepted refutation which was 17 ♘d5 ♖f7! 18 ♖ad1 e5 19 ♗g5 ♕e6 20 ♔h1 ♖af8 21 ♕h5 f4 22 ♖g1 e3 ∓ Ladbischensky - Lipnitsky, Harkov 1948, when Black's strong central pawns provide more than adequate compensation for White's extra piece.

17 ...   ♖f7
Domnitz - Kraidman, Tel Aviv 1964, continued 18 ♖g1 ♘e5 19 ♘d5 ♕d7 20 ♘d4 ♘g6 21 ♖xg6! hg 22 ♖g1 e5 23 ♖xg6! ♕d8 (23 ... ed 24 ♗xd4) 24 ♗g5 ♕a5 25 ♘f6+ ♔f8 26 ♘e6+ and White was winning.

C2:

11 ...   ♗g4

Or 11 ... ♖d8 12 ♖d1 ♘b4! 13 ♘d4 ♗c4 14 a3 ±; but the text is weak because of:
12 ♗d3! ±

11 ...   ♘b4
12 ♘d4   ♗c4
13 a3   ♗×e2
14 ♕×e2 ♘c6
15 ♖ad1

Black was threatening 15 ... ♘×e4

15 ♘b3 leaves White weak on the long diagonal after 15 ... ♘g4 16 ♗d2 a5 17 ♘d5 a4 ∓ - Koblencs.

15 ...   ♘g4!

Also possible is 15 ... ♖e8!
16 ♘d5   ♘×e3
17 ♕×e3 ♕d8
18 c3   e6 =
- Koblencs.

C4:

11 ...   a5!
12 a4

Not 12 ♘d4? ♘×e4! 13 ♘×c6 ♕×c6 14 ♗b5 ♗×c3 15 ♗×c6 ♗×e1 16 ♗×b7 ♗d2! winning, Durao - Levy, Praia da Rocha 1969.

12 ...   ♘b4
13 ♘d4   ♗c4
14 f5   ♘d7 =

Pachman - Gadalinsky, Spindleruv Mlyn 1948.

D:

11 h3

Preventing Black's ... ♘g4 and ... ♗g4, but Black has now two satisfactory lines: playing for an early ... d5 or creating queen's side play with ... a5.

D1: 11 ... ♘e8?
D2: 11 ... ♖d8
D3: 11 ... a5

D1:

11 ... ♘e8? is an unthematic alternative which aims to create play on the king's side. After 12 ♕d2 f5 13 ef gf 14 ♖ae1 ♔h8 15 ♘d4 ♗g8 16 g4! White has a distinct plus, Réti - Tartakower, New York 1924.

'The logical outcome of the last moves by Black, for White was already threatening to become dangerous with 13 g4, but the opening of new lines is favourable to White for the simple reason that he is better developed'. - Alekhine.

D2:

11 ...   ♖d8 (50)

50
W

This prepares ... d5, which would liquidate the centre by a series of exchanges and thus reduce the material with which White could operate on the king's side.

12 ♗f3
The most effective way of delaying ... d5. None of White's alternatives are any better:
a) 12 g4? d5 13 e5 ♘e4 14 ♘xe4 (14 ♕e1 f6!; or 14 ♗d3 f5!) 14 ... de 15 ♕e1 f6! ∓ - Koblencs.
b) 12 ♕e1 d5 13 e5 d4 14 ef ♗xf6 15 ♘e4 de 16 ♘xf6+ ef 17 ♗d3 ½-½ Eisinger-Rabar, Marienbad 1960.
c) 12 ♗d3 d5 13 e5 d4 14 ef ♗xf6 15 ♘e4 de 16 ♘xf6+ ef 17 ♖f3 (17 ♕e1 transposes to b) 17 ... ♗xb3 18 ab ♖e8 ∓ Blau-Rabar, Switzerland - Yugoslavia 1950.
d) 12 ♔h2? d5 13 e5 ♘e4 14 ♘b5 g5! ∓ A.R.B.Thomas - Flohr, Bournemouth 1939.
e) 12 ♘d4 ♘xd4 (12 ... ♗d7 is passive, e.g. 13 g4 ♘xd4 14 ♗xd4 ♗c6 - Lohmann - Bogoljubow, Bad Pyrmont 1949 - 15 ♗f3 ±) 13 ♗xd4 ♗c4 14 f5 d5 (Black must play actively in view of the threat of g4-g5) 15 e5 ♘e4 16 f6 ef 17 ef ♗f8 18 ♗xc4 ♕xc4 19 ♕d3 = Geller - Lipnitsky, ½F 18th USSR Ch 1950.

12 ... ♗c4
a) 12 ... ♘d7? allows White to sacrifice a pawn for a terrific bind by 13 ♘d5 ♗xb2 14 ♖b1 ♗g7 15 c4 ±; Gufeld gives 13 ♕d2 ♘c5 14 ♕f2

confining Black to passive defence.
b) 12 ... d5 leads to obscure complications which seem to turn out in White's favour; there are two plausible lines:
b1) 13 e5! and now:
b11) 13 ... d4 14 ♘xd4 ♘xd4 15 ♗xd4 ♕c4 16 ♘e2 ♘d5 17 ♗xd5 ♗xd5 18 c3 ♕c6 19 ♖f2 e6 20 ♘g3 ♖d7 21 ♘f1! ♖ad8 22 ♘e3 ♗e4 23 ♕g4 ♗f5 24 ♕h4 b5 25 g4! ± Pachman-Cajk, Czechoslovakia 1944.
b12) 13 ... ♘e4 14 ♘e2 (14 ♗xe4 de =) 14 ... g5! 15 fg ♗xe5 16 ♕c1 ♘d6 17 c3 ♘c4 18 ♗f4 ♕c7 19 ♗h5 ♕b6+ 20 ♔h1 h5 21 ♗xe5 ♘6xe5 (21 ... ♘4xe5 22 ♕f4 ±) 22 ♘bd4 and White, who is leading up to a strong attack with ♘g3 and ♘gf5, has the advantage, e.g.: 22 ... ♕xb2 23 ♕xb2 ♘xb2 24 ♖ab1 ±.
b2) 13 ed!? ♘b4 14 de ♖xd1 15 ef+ ♔xf7 16 ♖axd1 ♘xc2 17 ♗c5 a5! 18 ♘a4 ♕c7 19 ♖d2 ♘b4 20 ♖e1 ♖e8 = Rumens-Parma, Basle 1959.
b3) 13 ♘xd5 ♘xd5 14 ed ♘b4 =.
c) 12 ... a5 13 a4 ♗c4 14 ♖f2 e5 is considerably inferior to the text because in this instance (Black's rook on d8 presents a target, and White

has the move ♗b6 at his disposal.) Nilsson-Engels, Munich 1936, continued 15 ♗e2 d5? (15 ... ♗e6 16 ♗b6 ±) 16 ♗b6! ♗×e2 17 ♖×e2 ♖d7 18 ♘c5 ±±.

13 ♖f2

This move, intending to transfer the rook to the queen's file, is much better than the aimless 13 ♖e1, e.g. 13 ... d5 14 ed (14 e5 ♗×b3 15 ab d4 ∓) 14 ... ♘b4 15 ♗d4 ♘b×d5 16 ♘×d5 ♗×d5 17 c3 e6 18 ♗×d5 ♖×d5 19 ♕e2 ♕d7 ∓ Ary-Sentil, Brazilian Ch 1960.

13 ...   e5!

Less dynamic is 13 ... d5, e.g.

a) **14 e5?** ♗×b3 15 ab d4 16 ♖d2 dc 17 ♖×d8+ ♘×d8 18 ef cb 19 fe ♘c6 20 ♖b1 ♘×e7 ∓

b) **14 ed** ♘×d5 15 ♘×d5 ♗×d5 16 ♗×d5 e6 17 ♖d2 ♖×d5 18 ♖×d5 ed 19 c3 followed by ♕f3 and ♖d1 with advantage to White.

14 ♖d2

a) **14 f5** gf 15 ef d5 16 ♗g5 e4 gave Black a good game in Steinmeyer - Benko, US Ch 1962-3.

b) **14 fe** ♘×e5 clearly eases Black's task.

14 ...   ♕e6 *(51)*

Preparing ... d5 as well as defending the d-pawn.

a) On **14 ... ♕c7**, 15 ♕e1 followed by ♕h4 is the correct

way for White to proceed. If instead White tries to take direct advantage of Black's weak d5 square by 15 ♘d5, Black can switch his activities to the king's side where it is White who has several weak squares. Tarjan-Fazekas, corres, continued: 15 ♘d5 ♘×d5 16 ed ♘e7 17 fe ♗×e5 18 c3 ♘f5 ∓

b) A possibly playable alternative is **14 ... ef** 15 ♗×f4 ♘e5 16 ♔h2 (obviously not 16 ♖×d6 ♘×f3+ 17 gf ♖×d6 18 ♕×d6 ♕×h3 ∓∓) 16 ... ♕e6 (16 ... ♗a6, Matanović - Geller, Yugoslavia - USSR 1956, and 16 ... ♘e8 are also good) 17 g3 ♖d7 18 ♕h1 ♖ad8 19 ♖ad1 b6 20 ♘d4 ♕e8 Reuel-Bruggemann, corres 1959.

15 ♘d5

A new idea is 15 ♕e1 ef 16 ♗×f4 ♘e5 17 ♕g3 ♘×f3+ 18 ♕×f3 d5 Ornstein-Heim, Kringsja 1978.

15 ...   ef!

16 ♘d4

Instead:

a) 16 ♘c7 is clearly out of the question because of 16 ... ♕e5.
b) 16 ♘×f4 ♕e7 is perfectly satisfactory for Black. In view of what happens in the text, recapturing the pawn in relatively best, but Black has a good game.
c) 16 ♗×f4 ♘×e4 17 ♘c7 ♕f5 18 ♗×e4 ♕×f4 (19 ♘×a8 ♕×e4 20 ♘c7 ♗e5!) and again Black has a good game.

16 ...   ♘×d4
17 ♗×d4   ♗×d5
18 ed   ♕f5

White's pawn sacrifice has not turned out too well. True, Black's extra pawn is doubled, but it dominates two important squares and the 4:2 king's side majority is potentially strong for the end game. Rolland-Larsen, Le Havre 1966 continued: 19 ♖e2 h5 20 ♖e7 ♘d7 21 ♗×g7 ♔×g7 22 ♕d4+ ♕f6 23 ♖e4 ♖fc8 (With an extra pawn and the knight v bad bishop complex, Black is ideally situated for the ensuing endgame.) 24 c3 ♕×d4+ 25 ♖×d4 ♘e5 26 ♗e2 ♖c5 27 ♖ad1 (Because of the threat to his f-pawn, Black is forced to exchange a king's side pawn for one in the centre, leaving his queen's pawn a little weak.) 27 ... g5 28 ♗×h5 ♘c4 29 ♖e1 ♘e3 30 ♗d1 ♖×d5 31 ♖×d5 ♘×d5 32 ♗f3 ♘e3 33 ♖e2 d5! 34 c4 dc 35 ♖d2 ♖c8 36 ♗×b7 c3 37 bc ♖×c3 38 ♔f2 f5 39 a4 a5 40 h4? (On the last move of the time control White finds a faulty plan which only hastens his demise.) 40 ... g4 41 ♖d4 (The point of his last move.) 41 ... ♖c2+ 42 ♔e1 ♖b2 0-1.

D3:
11 ...   a5 *(52)*

52
W

This active thrust which is mentioned only *en passant* in the 10th edition of *MCO*, constitutes Black's most forceful plan in the Classical Dragon. The ideas have been seen before in variations B, chapter 3, and E2, chapter 7. Here we augment the details to illustrate Black's potential in the position of diagram 52. White can now consider:
D31: 12 a3
D32: 12 a4
D33: 12 ♗f3
D34: 12 ♘d5?
D35: 12 ♘a4?

D36: 12 ♘d4!

D31:
  12 a3 a4 13 ♘d2 d5 14 e5 d4 15 ef ef 16 ♗xd4 ♘xd4 ∓

D32:
  12 a4   ♘b4
  13 ♖c1
  Black was threatening 13 ... ♘xe4 14 ♘xe4 ♘xc2; other White tries are:
  a) 13 ♘d4 ♗c4 14 f5 ♘d7 15 fg hg 16 ♔h1 ♘e5 17 h4? ♗xe2 18 ♕xe2 ♕g4! 19 ♘f3 ♖ac8 ∓ Erny-Parma, Basle 1959.
  b) 13 ♗f3 ♘d7 14 ♘d4 ♗c4 15 ♖f2 ♖d8 16 ♘d5 ♗xd5 17 ed ♘b6 18 ♘c6? ♘bxd5! 19 c4?? ♘xe3! 20 ♘xe7+ ♔f8 21 ♕e2 ♕c5 0-1, Van Hombeek - Nikitin, 1960.
  c) Best is 13 ♗d4 ♗c4, when Black's chances for an advantage have been minimized.
    13 ...   ♘d7
  Momo-Nikitin, Leningrad 1960, continued: 14 ♗d4 ♗xb3 15 cb ♗xd4+ 16 ♕xd4 ♕c5 17 ♖fd1 ♕xd4+ 18 ♖xd4 ♘c5 19 ♗c4 ♖ac8 20 f5 ♘d7 21 fg hg 22 ♘d5 ♘xd5 23 ♖xd5 ♘c5 24 ♖e1 b6, and Black has a good knight v bad bishop ending.

D33:
  12 ♗f3   a4!

  13 ♘d4   a3!
  14 b3   ♘e5!
- Koblencs, 15 ef ♕xc3 16 ♕e1 ♕xe1 17 ♖axe1 de ∓.

D34:
  12 ♘d5?   ♗xd5
  13 ed   ♘b4
  14 c4   a4
  15 ♘d4
  Or 15 a3 ♘fxd5!! 16 cd ♘c2 17 ♕d3 ab and now:
  a) 18 ♖ac1 ♗xb2 19 ♕xb3 ♗xc1 20 ♖xc1 ♘d4!!
  b) 18 ♖ab1 ♕f5 19 ♕xf5 (19 ♕xb3 ♕e4!) 19 ... gf 20 ♗b6 ♖fc8 21 ♖f3 ♗d4+ with a won ending for Black, Roose-Kramer, Baarn 1940.
    15 ...   a3 ∓
  Cortlever - Fontein, Amsterdam 1939.

D35:
  12 ♘a4?   ♗xb3!
  13 ab
  a) 13 cb ♕e6! 14 e5 ♘fd5 15 ♗c1 de ∓.
  b) 13 ♘b6? ♕e6 14 ♘xa8 ♕xe4 15 ♕d3 ♗xc2 16 ♕xe4 ♘xe4 17 ♖ac1 ♘g3! ∓ - Koblencs.
    13 ...   ♕e6!
  Not 13 ... ♘xe4? 14 ♘b6 ♕e6 15 ♗c4! ± - Zhdanov.
  14 ♗c4   ♕xe4
  15 ♖e1 ♘b4! 16 ♖e2 ♕c6 17 ♘b6 ♖ad8 18 ♖xa5 d5! 19 ♗b5 ♕c7 20 ♗d4 ♘h5!

∓ Bogoljubow - Herrmann, Lünburg 1947.

D36:

12 ♘d4! ♘xd4
13 ♗xd4 ♗c4
14 ♗d3 e5!
15 fe

Or 15 ♗e3 ef 16 ♗xf4 d5! O'Hanlon - Cortlever, Buenos Aires 1939.

15 ... de
15 ♗e3

Naturally White cannot capture the e-pawn because of 16 ... ♕c5+ 17 ♔h1 ♗xd3 and 18 ... ♕xe5.

16 ... ♕c6
17 ♗g5 ♘h5 =

So far Alexander-Euwe, The Hague 1939, and Fink-Estrin, corres 1960. The second of these continued: 18 ♗xc4 ♕xc4 19 ♕d5 ♕xd5 20 ♘xd5 f6 21 ♗h4 ♖f7 22 ♘b6 ♖a6 23 ♗f2 f5 24 ♖ad1 ♘f4 25 ♖d8+ ♖f8 26 ♖fd1 ♘e2+ 27 ♔f1 ½-½. 27 ... ♘d4 28 ♖xf8+ ♗xf8 would probably have been the continuation.

Levenfish – Introduction

1 e4 c5 2 ♘f3 d6 3 d4 cd 4 ♘×d4 ♘f6 5 ♘c3 g6 6 f4 *(53)*

53
B

The move 6 f4 was first seen in the game Levenfish - Rabinovich, 11th USSR Ch 1936. The idea was to refute the obvious 6 ... ♗g7 by advancing immediately in the centre with 7 e5, and for almost forty years theory accepted Levenfish's original conception. Between 1936 and the mid 1950's Levenfish analysed and played the variation which had quickly come to bear his name, and even today the move 6 f4 is not without its sting.

When writing the first edition of *The Sicilian Dragon*, I was of the opinion that 6 ... ♘bd7 was Black's best counter. The move had been tried with some success by the young English players during the 1960's and little evidence had come to light to suggest a refutation. Now I am of a completely different opinion: I believe that Black's reply to 6 f4 should be 6 ... ♗g7, the very move that Levenfish sought to refute, while I also believe that 6 ... ♘c6, which was condemned in my earlier works, can be made playable by substituting 10 ... ♗e7 (variation B431) for the refuted 10 ... ♕e7.

In this chapter we shall examine the rarely seen 6 ... ♘bd7 and a couple of other useless alternatives.

6 ...   ♘bd7 *(54)*

This move must still be regarded as experimental. Other tries are:

a) **6 ... ♗g4** 7 ♗b5+ (7 ♕d3 ♘c6 8 ♗e3 ♗g7 9 h3 ♗d7 10 ♗e2 is good for White in view of the possible pawn-storm g4-g5 and h4. Sherwin - D.Byrne, New York 1955.) 7 ... ♘bd7 8 ♗×d7+ ♕×d7 (8 ... ♗×d7 9 e5!) 9 ♕d3 e5 10 ♘f3 ♗×f3 11 ♕×f3 ♕g4? (11 ... ef 12 ♗×f4 ♗g7 and 13 ... 0-0 was better.) 12 ♘d5! 1-0?! Korchnoi - Spassky, USSR Junior Ch 1948. Spassky overlooked the fact that he could prolong the game by 12 ... ♔d8 although after 13 ♕×g4 (13 ♘×f6? ♕h4+) 13 ... ♘×g4 14 h3 ♘h6 15 fe de 16 ♗g5+ ♔c8 17 ♗f6, Black has no hope of salvation.

b) In the first edition of *The Sicilian Dragon* 6 ... ♕b6 was mentioned in print for the first time. It was put in as an after-thought with little analysis to support it.

White must be careful not to over-extend himself in attempts at outright refutation, despite the following: **7 e5** de 8 fe ♘fd7 (8 ... ♘g4? 9 ♗b5+) 9 e6! (9 ♗f4 ♗g7 10 ♗c4 ♘×e5 11 ♘d5 ♕c5 12 ♘b5 0-0 13 ♗×e5 ♗×e5 14 ♕e2 ♘c6 15 b4 ♘×b4 16 ♕×e5 ♘×c2+ 17 ♔d2 ♖d8! ∓ Allison-Glazer, USA 1971) 9 ... fe 10 ♗c4 ♘c6 11 ♘×e6 ♘de5? 12 ♘d5! ♕a5+ 13 b4 ♘×b4 14 ♘dc7+ ♔f7 15 0-0+ ±± Kopche-Schelbhorn, Hamburg 1973.

White's best course may be

7 ♗e2 ♘c6 8 ♗e3 and if 8 ... e5 then 9 fe de 10 ♘×c6! winning a piece.

Also good is **7 ♗e3** e5 8 fe de 9 ♗b5+ ♘c6 10 ♘f5 ♕c7 11 ♗g5!

c) **6 ... a6** transposes to a line of the Najdorf variation that is rather good for White: 7 ♘f3 ♗g7 8 e5 ♘g4 (8 ... de 9 ♕×d8+ ♔×d8 10 fe ♘g4 11 ♗f4 ±) 9 h3 ♘h6 10 ♗c4 0-0 11 g4 ♘c6 12 ♗e3 de 13 fe ±

6 ... ♗g7! is chapter 12, page 103.

6 ... ♘c6 is chapter 11, page 83.

54
W

6 ... ♘bd7 is Flohr's recommendation which, quite unjustifiably, is most rare in master chess. Perhaps the worst that can befall Black is a transposition to lines of the 6 f4 attack against the Najdorf Variation (5 ... a6) with the option of delaying the move ... a6 to a more propitious moment. Opening literature has underestimated this move but the following suggestions should set it on the path to full rehabilitation.

7 ♗e2

a) 7 ♗c4 is easy to meet, e.g.

a1) 7 ... ♗g7 8 ♗e3 0-0 9 h3 a6 10 a4 ♕c7 = Rossetto-Najdorf, Mar del Plata 1968.

a2) 7 ... ♕c7 8 ♗b3 a6 9 0-0 ♗g7 10 ♗e3 b5 11 ♕f3 ♗b7 = Fazekas-Wood, Bognor Regis 1960.

b) 7 ♘f3 and now 7 ... ♕c7 (preventing Parma's suggestion of 8 ♗c4 to strengthen the threat of e5 at some stage) 8 ♗d3 ♗g7 9 0-0 0-0 10 ♕e1 a6 11 ♔h1 b5 12 e5? de 13 fe ♘g4 14 e6 ♘c5 ∓ Andersson-R.Garcia, Skopje OL 1972.

If Black replies to 7 ♘f3 with 7 ... ♗g7, White must be careful not to play e5 too soon, e.g.: 8 e5 de 9 fe ♘g4 10 e6 fe 11 ♘g5 ♗×c3+ 12 bc ♕a5 13 ♕×g4 ♕×c3+ 14 ♔d1 ♕×a1 ∓/∓∓ Fernandez - Barczay, Budapest 1978.

7 ... ♗g7
8 ♗e3

If White behaves too optimistically on the K-side he could be crushed in the centre. Tuomainen - Lee, Cracow 1964, went: 8 ♗f3 0-0 9 g4? e5! 10 ♘db5 d5! 11 ed e4 12 ♗e2 ♘b6 (threatening 13 ... ♘×g4) 13 g5 ♘f×d5 14 ♘×e4 ♕e7 15 ♘f2 ♖e8 with Black well on the way to victory;

the game concluded 16 ♕f1 a6? (16 ... ♗×b2 17 ♗×b2 ♘e3+ or 17 ♖b1 ♗×c1 wins quicker) 17 ♘d6 (17 ♘a3 ♗×b2) 17 ... ♕×d6 18 c4 ♖×e2 19 ♕×e2 ♘×f4 20 ♕f3 ♘e6 21 ♔g2 ♘×c4 22 ♘e4 ♕c7 23 ♘f6+ ♗×f6 24 gf ♗d7! 25 0-1.

The most satisfactory alternative is 8 0-0 0-0 and now:

a) 9 ♔h1 a6 10 ♗f3 e5 11 ♘de2 ef 12 ♕×d6 g5! 13 e5 ♘e8 14 ♕d3 ♕e7 15 ♘d5 ♕c5 16 ♕f5 ♘b6 and White was soon crushed, Eley - Whiteley, British Ch, Blackpool 1971.

b) 9 ♗f3 with:

b1) 9 ... e5 10 ♘db5 ♕b6+ (10 ... ♘e8 11 ♔h1 ef 12 ♗×f4 ± is better) 11 ♔h1 ♘e8 12 a4 a6 13 ♘d5 ♕d8 14 ♘bc3 ef 15 ♗×f4 ♘e5 16 a5 ± or 16 ♗e2 ± - Miles.

b2) 9 ... a6 10 ♘b3 ♘b6 (If 10 ... ♕b6+ 11 ♔h1 e5 12 f5 followed by g4-g5; but possibly stronger than the text is 10 ... ♕c7 11 g4 ♘b6) 11 a4 (11 g4!?) 11 ... ♗e6 12 a5 ♘c4 13 g4 ♖b8 (better 13 ... b5!?) 14 f5 ♗d7 15 ♗e2 b5 16 g5 ♘e8 17 ♘d4 (if 17 ♘d5 ♗e5 followed by ... ♘c7 or e6) 17 ... ♘c7 18 h4 ♘e5 19 ♗e3 ± Eley-Miles, Birmingham 1973.

b3) Best of all is 9 ... ♘b6 when 10 e5 leads to interesting

possibilities for both sides.
   Finally, Black can meet 8 0-0 with **8 ... a6**, deferring castling, e.g.: 9 a4 (9 ♔h1 0-0 transposes to (a) above) 9 ... 0-0 10 ♗f3 (10 ♘b3 b6 11 ♗f3 ♗b7 ∞ - Geller) 10 ... e5! 11 ♘b3 ef (11 ... ♕c7 12 f5! ±) 12 ♗×f4 ♘e5 13 ♗g5 ♕b6+ 14 ♔h1 ♗e6 ∞ - Geller.

8 ... 0-0
9 ♗f3 ♘b6

Horowitz - Reshevsky, New York 1944, went 9 ... a6 10 0-0 ♕c7 11 ♔h1 ♖b8? 12 a4 b6? 13 e5 de 14 ♘c6 and White won material. Up to now all these moves have been uncritically accepted by the theoreticians, but in 1944 Boleslavsky had not yet exported his ... e5 beyond the borders of Muscovy. With modern technique added we find that 11 ... e5! 12 ♘b3 b5 allows Black to achieve an excellent position analogous to situations that might arise after White had badly misplayed a 6 f4 attack against the Najdorf. In this position the backward d-pawn is not a liability.

10 ♕e2 e5
11 ♘b3 *(55)*

Tolush - Abramian, Leningrad 1939. The evaluation (±) is the common verdict; but authorities such as Koblenz do not support the judgement with any analysis.
   In my opinion Black has a

55
B

plethora of dynamic possibilities available, e.g.

a) **11 ... ♗e6** discouraging White from castling K-side, while preparing to occupy the c4 square.

b) **11 ... ♘g4** threatening to exchange White's QB and containing the idea of ... ef followed by ... ♘e5. (Possibly this tactical device was unknown in 1939 but it has become common knowledge from lines of the King's Indian.) Play might continue 12 ♗×g4 ♕h4+ 13 g3 ♕×g4 14 ♕×g4 ♗×g4 (analysis by Keene) when Black's two bishops, better development and threat of ... ♘c4 give him a fully satisfactory position.

c) The adventurous **11 ... ef** 12 ♗×f4 ♘h5 13 ♗×h5 ♕h4+ 14 ♗g3 ♕×h5 15 ♕×h5 gh 16 ♗×d6 ♖e8 when Black will regain the pawn with an equal position; perhaps White does better to spurn the pawn with 16 0-0-0 though he may then subject himself to serious pressure after 16 ... ♖d3 f5 (19 h3 fe) - analysis by ♗g4 17 ♖×d6 ♘c4 18 Keene and Levy.

11 Levenfish with 6 ... ♘c6

1 e4 c5 2 ♘f3 d6 3 d4 cd 4 ♘×d4 ♘f6 5 ♘c3 g6 6 f4 6 ... 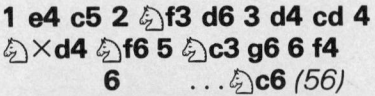♘c6 (56)

56
W

For many years most theoretical manuals considered this to be the only serious reply at Black's disposal. In the first and second editions of my Batsford book *The Sicilian Dragon*, I demonstrated that the main line, involving a supposedly equalising manoeuvre invented by Eliskases, was rather worse for Black than had previously been supposed. At the time of writing the present volume I still hold this view, but I have revised my assessment of 10 ... ♗e7 (variation B431, page 9, and now consider this move to be the main line, and a satisfactory one for Black.

The move 6 ... ♘c6 is not without importance in Dragon theory, even though 6 ... ♗g7 is probably a better choice. The reason for the importance of 6 ... ♘c6 lies in the transpositional possibility 1 e4 c5 2 ♘f3 ♘c6 (or 2 ... d6) 3 d4 cd 4 ♘×d4 ♘f6 5 ♘c3 d6 (or 5 ... ♘c6) 6 f4, when Black may, if he wishes, avoid the Scheveningen set-up of 6 ... e6 and instead opt for the Dragon move 6 ... g6.
A: 7 ♗b5
B: 7 ♘×c6

After **7 ♘f3** ♗g4 8 h3 (8 ♗e3 or 8 ♗e2 are both stronger) 8 ... ♗×f3 9 ♕×f3 ♗g7 10 ♗e3 0-0 and now:
a) 11 ♖d1 ♕a5 12 a3 ♖ac8 13 ♗e2 ♘d7 ∓ Evans - Reshevsky, New York 1954.
b) 11 ♗e2 ♘d7 12 ♖d1 ♕a5 13 h4 h5 14 e5 ♘b6 15 ed ed 16 0-0 = Seidman-Evans, US Open 1955.

7 ♗e2 or **7 ♗e3** will simply

transpose into the Classical Dragon.

A:

7 ♗b5 *(57)*

57 B

Botvinnik's move, which was successfully adopted by Penrose during the mid-1950's. The problems posed in this line are not sufficiently wide-ranging and against accurate defence White can expect no more than equality.

   7 ...   ♗d7

This is solid but less likely to usurp the initiative than 7 ... ♕c7! after which:

a) **8 ♘d5** releases the tension prematurely, as shown in analysis by Pachman, viz. 8 ... ♘×d5 9 ed a6 and now:

a1) **10 ♗×c6+** bc 11 ♘×c6 ♗g7 12 ♗e3 ♗b7 13 ♗d4 ♗×d4 14 ♕×d4 0-0 15 0-0 ♗×c6 = Schmid - Parma, Malaga 1963.

a2) **10 ♗a4?** ♕a5+ 11 c3 ♕×d5 12 ♘×c6 ♕×d1+ 13 ♔×d1 ♗d7 wins a pawn.

a3) **10 ♘×c6** ab 11 ♕d4 e5!

12 de ♕×c6 13 ♕×h8 ♕×g2 and Black is probably winning, e.g. 14 ef+ ♔×f7 15 ♖f1 ♗h3 or 14 ♖f1 ♗×e6 when White's king is fatally exposed.

b) **8 ♗e3** is not recommended on account of 8 ... ♗d7 9 ♘d5 ♘×d5 10 ed ♘b4! 11 ♗×d7+ ♕×d7 12 ♘f3 ♕f5 when Black wins material.

c) **8 0-0** ♗d7 is at least as good for Black as the main line, since after 9 ♗×c6 bc, 10 e5 is no longer possible, while 9 ♘d5 ♘×d5 10 ed ♘×d4 11 ♗×d7+ ♔×d7 12 ♕×d4 ♕c5 results in a completely drawn ending.

   8 ♗×c6

8 ♘f3 allows the equalising 8 ... ♗g4, analogous to Seidman-Evans in the note to 7 ♘f3.

After 8 ♗×c6 Black has the choice of:
A1: 8 ... bc
A2: 8 ... ♗×c6

A1:

   8 ...   bc *(58)*
   9 e5

and now:
A11: 9 ... ♘g4??
A12: 9 ... ♘d5
A13: 9 ... de

A11:

   9 ... ♘g4?? loses a piece after 10 e6 fe 11 ♕×g4 e5 12

11 Levenfish with 6 ... ♘c6

58
W

♘e6 ♕c8 13 f5 (13 ... gf 14 ♕h5++).

A12:

    9 ...   **♘d5**

Until recently I considered this move to be much better than its reputation, but now I am not so sure.

    10 ed

If 10 ♘xd5 cd 11 ♕f3 (11 ed e6 ∓, but 11 0-0 ♗g7 12 ♕f3 e6 transposes) 11 ... e6 12 0-0 (or 12 ♗d2 de 13 fe ♕h4+ 14 ♕f2 ♕e4+ 15 ♕e3 ♕xe3+ 16 ♗xe3 ♗g7 17 ♘f3 0-0 18 ♗d4 ♖fc8 19 0-0-0 ♗b5 20 ♖he1 a5 = Chaplinsky - Tolush, 20th USSR Ch 1952.) 12 ... ♗g7 13 c3! (This new move of Olafsson's is stronger than 13 ♗d2 ♕b6 14 ♗c3 0-0 15 ♖ae1 de 16 fe f6 ∓) 13 ... 0-0 14 ♕g3 ♕c7 15 ed ♕xd6 16 ♗e3 a5 17 ♖ad1 ♖ab8 18 ♖f2 a4 19 a3 ♖b7 20 h4 ♖fb8 21 ♖dd2 f6 22 ♘f3 ♕e7 23 ♗d4 ± Olafsson - Panchenko, Las Palmas 1978.

    10 ...   **♘xc3**
    11 bc   **c5!**

Not 11 ... ed 12 0-0 ♗e7 13 f5! 0-0 14 ♗h6 ♖e8 15 fg followed by 16 ♕f3 ± - Levenfish.

    12 ♘f3

Interesting is 12 de ♕xe7+ 13 ♘e2 ♖d8 14 ♕d3 ♗c6 15 ♕g3? (15 ♕e3 ∓) 15 ... ♗g7 16 0-0 as in M.Johansson - Nilsson, Stockholm 1960-61, when 16 ... ♕xe2 would have won a piece.

    12 ...   **♗g7!**

Nilsson's move.

    13 ♘e5

If 13 0-0 0-0 14 de ♕xe7 15 ♖e1 ♗e6, when Black has the two bishops and a strong king position while White has a poor pawn structure.

    13 ...   **♗b5**
    14 c4

Or 14 ♖b1 ♗a6 15 ♕d5 0-0 ∓

    14 ...   **ed!**
    15 cb

The position is roughly equal. Analysis by Nilsson.

A13:

    9 ...   **de**
    10 fe   **♘g4** *(59)*

10 ... ♘d5 is not playable because of 11 ♘xd5 cd 12 ♕f3!

After 10 ... ♘g4 there is:
A131: 11 ♗f4
A132: 11 e6?!

11 Levenfish with 6 ... ♘c6

59
W

11 ♘×c6?? backfires after 11 ... ♕b6

A131:
11 ♗f4

Since the sacrifice 11 e6 is of dubious merit, this may be White's best line.

11 ...   ♗g7
12 ♕e2   ♕a5

12 ... ♕b8 13 0-0-0 ♗×e5 14 ♗g5! ♗f4+? (14 ... f6 or 14 ... h6 would have been better, though then White would have ample compensation for the pawn.) 15 ♗×f4 ♕×f4+ 16 ♔b1 ♕e5 17 ♕a6 ♕c7 18 ♖he1 ♘e5 19 ♕a3! ± Schmid - Gilg, Düsseldorf 1951.

13 ♘f3   ♕b4!

Black has good counterplay - Euwe.

The text is considerably stronger than 13 ... 0-0 14 h3 ♗h6 15 ♗×h6 ♘×h6 16 ♕d2 ♘f5 17 ♕×d7 winning a piece.

A132:
11 e6?!   ♗×e6

12 ♕f3

This preparation for Q-side castling is an idea of the Tartar International Master, Nezhmetdinov.

White could play more circumspectly with 12 ♘×e6 ♕×d1+ 13 ♘×d1 fe 14 ♘e3 ♘f6 15 ♘c4 ♘d5 16 ♗d2 ♗g7 17 0-0-0 ♖f8 18 ♖hf1 0-0-0 19 ♘a5 ♔c7 20 c4 ♘b6 = Geller - Pogrebisky, 17th USSR Ch 1949.

12 ...   ♕d7

This is the only way to defend everything. If 12 ... ♘e5 13 ♕e4.

13 ♗f4   ♗g7
14 0-0-0   ♗d5

Not 14 ... ♗×d4? 15 ♖×d4 ♕b7 16 h3 ♘f6 17 ♗h6! ±; nor 14 ... 0-0 ♘f5 ♕b7 16 ♘×g7 ♔×g7 17 h3 ♘f6 18 ♗e5 ±

15 ♕e2   ♘f6

If 15 ... 0-0 16 ♘×c6! ♕×c6 17 ♘×d5 etc.

16 ♗e5

The only way to maintain the pressure. If 16 ♖he1 simply 16 ... 0-0.

16 ...   0-0
17 ♗×f6   ef

If 17 ... ♗×f6 18 ♘×c6 ♕×c6 19 ♘×d5 ♗g5+ 20 ♔b1 e6 21 h4! ♗d8, Black's K-side is full of holes.

18 ♘×c6   ♕×c6
19 ♘×d5 ♖fe8 20 ♕f3 (20 ♘e7+?? ♔f8) 20 ... ♖ac8

11 Levenfish with 6 ... ♘c6

21 c3 f5 22 ♖he1 ♔f8 when, according to Euwe, Black has a satisfactory position.

A2:

8 ... ♗×c6 *(60)*

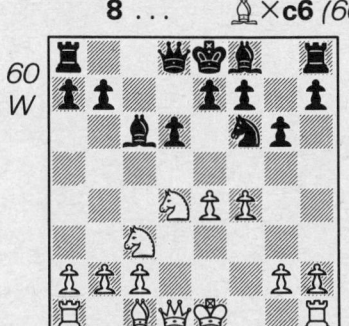

Now:
A21: 9 ♕e2
A22: 9 ♕f3
A23: 9 e5

A21:

9 ♕**e2** is one possibility which has not been tested, but against this move Black should not have anything to fear, e.g. 9 ... ♗g7 10 ♘×c6 bc 11 e5 de 12 fe ♘d5.

A22:

9 ♕**f3** *(61)*
and now:
a) 9 ... ♕**b6** 10 ♘×c6 (if 10 ♘b3 ♘×e4! 11 ♘×e4 ♕b4+ 12 ♘bd2 f5) 10 ... ♕×c6 (on 10 ... bc? comes 11 e5 de 12 fe ♘d7 13 e6 fe 14 ♖f1 0-0-0 15 ♗e3 and White will have more than enough compensation for the sacrificed pawn - Levenfish.) 11 ♗e3 ♗g7 12 0-0 0-0 = Shmit-Kogan, 1964.
b) 9 ... ♖**c8** 10 ♗e3 ♗g7 11 0-0-0 0-0 12 g4 ♕c7 13 h4 (13 ♖d2 maintains the balance.) 13 ... ♘×e4! 14 ♘×e4 f5 15 gf gf 16 ♘e6 ♗×e4 17 ♕×e4 fe 18 ♘×c7 ♖×c7 19 ♖hg1 ♔f7 20 ♗×a7 b6 21 ♗×b6 ♗×b2+ ∓ Klavin - Zaitsev, Vladimir 1962.
c) After 9 ... ♕**c7**, in Klavin-A.Geller, 1962 Latvian Ch, an almost identical position to (b) was reached by 10 ♗e3 ♗g7 11 0-0-0 0-0 12 g4 ♖fc8; now White won crushingly by 13 g5 ♘d7 (13 ... ♗×e4 14 ♕e2 ♗×h1 15 gf ♗×f6 16 ♖×h1 would have been infinitely better for Black than the text, though White would still have the advantage with his threats of 17 ♘d5 as well as h4-h5.) 14 h4 b5 15 ♖d2 ♘b6 16 h5 b4 17 hg hg 18 ♖dh2 ♔f8 19 f5 1-0.
d) 9 ... ♘**d7**! 10 ♘×c6 bc 11 e5 d5 ∓ - Geller.

11 Levenfish with 6 ... ♘c6

A23:

9 e5 *(62)*

9 ...   de
10 fe   ♘e4

Polyak-Tarasov, USSR 1953, went instead 10 ... ♘d5 11 e6! f5 12 0-0 ♘f6 (12 ... ♗g7 13 ♘xf5!) 13 ♘xc6 ♕xd1 14 ♖xd1 bc 15 ♗g5 ♗g7 16 ♗xf6 ♗xf6 17 ♖d7 0-0 when White could have kept his endgame advantage by 18 ♘a4 ♖fb8 19 c3.

11 ♘xe4

11 e6 would not be correct because of 11 ... fe! (Weaker is 11 ... f5 12 0-0 ♗g7 13 ♘xf5! ♗xc3 14 bc ♕xd1 15 ♘g7+ ♔d8 16 ♖xd1+ ♔c8? 17 ♗a3 ♖g8 18 ♖f1! ± Penrose - Wade, English County game 1956.) 12 ♘xc6 ♕xd1+ 13 ♘xd1 bc 14 0-0 ♗g7 when Black's active piece play provides more than sufficient compensation for his grotty pawn structure.

11 ♘xc6 is analysed by Levenfish as leading to the better endgame for White after 11 ... ♕xd1+ 12 ♘xd1 bc 13 0-0 ♗g7 14 ♖e1 ♘c5 15 ♗d2 but now, instead of 15 ... ♘d7 16 ♗c3, Black can improve with 15 ... 0-0 16 ♗b4 ♘d7 17 e6 (On 17 ♗xe7 ♖fe8 White loses his e-pawn.) 17 ... fe 18 ♗xe7 ♖fe8 19 ♗d6 ♘b6 with active piece play again providing Black with compensation for his sick pawns.

11 ...   ♗xe4
12 0-0   ♗g7
13 ♖e1?

We are following Penrose-Barden, Hastings 1957-8. Afterwards Penrose recommended 13 ♗f4 with chances for both players, e.g. 13 ... 0-0 14 c3 ♕b6 = - Geller.

13 ...   ♕d5

13 ... ♗c6 was tried in Kavalek-Jansa, Czech Ch 1962; the game continued 14 ♗g5! ♕b6 (not 14 ... 0-0 15 ♘xc6 bc 16 ♕xd8 and 17 ♗xe7) 15 c3 ♖d8 (15 ... ♕xb2 16 ♘xc6 bc 17 ♗xe7 ♔xe7 18 ♕d6+ ♔e8 19 e6 wins for White.) 16 ♕e2 ♖d5 17 ♗f6! 0-0 18 ♗xg7 ♔xg7 19 ♕f2 ♕c5 20 ♕g3 ♖fd8 21 ♖ad1 a5 22 ♖d3 b5 23 ♕f4 b4 24 ♔h1 bc 25 bc ♔g8 26 ♖h3, and Black had no defence to the threat of ♕h6.

13 ... ♗d5, on the other

11 Levenfish with 6 ... ♘c6

hand, leads to an equal position after 14 c3 0-0. White cannot afford to play 14 c4 ♗c6 (14 ... ♗×c4 15 ♕a4+ b5 16 ♘×b5 ♕b6+ 17 ♘d4+!) 15 ♗g5 because of 15 ... ♕b6 nor 15 e6 when Gufeld and Lazarev recommend 15 ... f5 with a positional plus for Black but I prefer 15 ... ♕×d4+ winning a piece.

14 c3   ♕×e5

This is forced. If instead Black tries

a) **14 ... 0-0** 15 ♕e2 ♗f5 16 ♘×f5 gf White can build up a K-side attack.

b) **14 ... ♗×e5**, the effective answer is 15 ♕a4+ ♔f8 16 ♖×e4.

c) **14 ... ♗×g2** 15 c4 wins.

15 ♗f4!

If **15 ♕e2** f5 16 ♗f4 ♕d5! (16 ... ♕f4? 17 ♕b5+ ♔f7 18 ♕c4+) 17 ♖ad1 0-0 and White's attacking chances are not worth a pawn.

Or **15 ♕a4+ ♗c6!**.

15 ...   ♕×f4

Not 15 ... ♕d5 16 ♕a4+!.

16 ♕a4+ *(63)*

16 ...   ♗c6?

The decisive error. **16 ... b5?** also loses, viz. 17 ♕×b5+ ♔f8 18 ♘e6+ fe 19 ♖f1 ♕×f1+ 20 ♖×f1+ ♗f6 21 ♕b4!

Best is **16 ... ♔f8!** when after 17 ♘e6+ fe 18 ♖f1 ♕×f1+ 19 ♖×f1+ ♗f5 20

g4 ♗f6 21 gf ef Black has excellent winning chances due to his strong K-side pawns.

17 ♖×e7+ ♔f8

18 ♘e6+ fe 19 ♕×f4+ ♔×e7 20 ♕c7+ ♗d7 21 ♖d1 ♖ad8 (not 21 ... ♖hd8 22 ♕×b7, threatening 23 ♖×d7+) 22 ♕×b7 ♖hf8 (22 ... a5 23 c4 ♔e8 24 c5 ♗e5 25 ♕b6 ♖b8 - 25 ... ♖c8 26 ♕×a5 ♗×b2 27 ♕d2 etc. - 26 ♕a7 ♗c6 27 ♖d6! ♖b7 28 ♕a6 ♗×d6 29 ♕×c6+ wins) 23 ♕×a7 (23 c4 ♖f4! and if 24 c5 ♗d4+) 23 ... ♖f5 24 a4 ♗e5 25 a5 ♔e8 26 a6 ♗c6 (If 26 ... ♗b5 27 ♖×d8+ ♔×d8 28 ♕a8+ ♔d7 29 ♕b7+ ♔d6 30 g4!) 27 ♖×d8+ ♔×d8 28 ♕e3 (after 28 ♕b6+ ♔d7 29 a7 ♖f8 White would have difficulty in advancing his other passed pawns. Also inferior would be 25 ♕×h7 because of 28 ... ♗c7 with some dangerous mating threats. The text centralises the queen and threatens 29 g4.) 28 ... ♗c7 29 b4

♖e5 30 ♕d4+ ♔c8 31 c4 ♖e4 32 ♕h8+ ♔d7 33 ♕×h7+ ♔d8 34 ♕g8+ ♔d7 35 ♕f7+ ♔c8 36 ♕f8+ ♗d8 (36 ... ♔d7 fails to 37 b5 ♗b6+ 38 c5 ♗×b5 39 ♕d6+) 37 ♕c5 ♔d7 38 b5 ♗a8 39 ♕a7+ 1-0, Penrose-Barden, Hastings 1957-8.

B:

7 ♘×c6! bc *(64)*

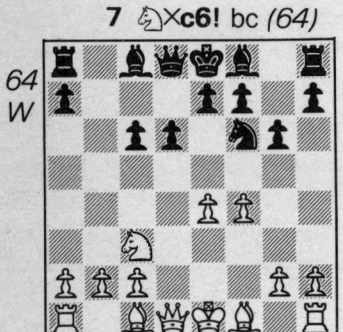

64
W

8 e5

This is White's only consistent follow-up. Now:
B1: 8 ... ♗g4
B2: 8 ... de
B3: 8 ... ♘g4
B4: 8 ... ♘d7

B1:

8 ... ♗g4, trying to make something of the principle that trading pieces usually helps the defender, fails here. After 9 ♗e2 ♗×e2 10 ♕×e2 de 11 fe ♘d5 White can get a terrific bind with 12 e6!, e.g. 12 ... f5 13 ♘×d5 (Not 13 ♕e5? ♘f6 14 ♗e3 ♗g7 15 ♖d1 ♕c8 as White's isolated pawn will soon fall.) 13 ... ♕×d5 14 ♗g5! followed by ♖d1 and ♖d7 at an opportune moment — Euwe.

B2:

8 ... de *(65)*

A move which leaves Black precariously placed.

65
W

9 ♕×d8+ ♔×d8
10 fe ♘g4

Black hopes that play against White's e-pawn will balance out the poor position of his king and his retarded development.

Other knight moves are weak:
a) **10 ... ♘d7** 11 ♗f4 ♗g7 12 0-0-0 ♔e8 13 ♖e1 ♘c5 14 ♗e2 ♗d7 15 ♗f3 ± - Fine.
b) **10 ... ♘d5?** and now:
b1) **11 ♗d2** ♔c7 (Or 11 ... ♗g7 12 0-0-0 ♗×e5 13 ♘×d5 cd 14 ♗a5+ ♔e8 15 ♖×d5 ♗f4+ 16 ♗d2 ♗e6 17 ♗b5+ ♔f8 18 ♖d3 ± Glass-Steiner, Austria 1962.) 12 0-0-0 ♘×c3 13 ♗×c3 ♗e6 14 ♖d4 ♗h6+ 15 ♔b1 ♗e3 16 ♖e4 ♗b6 17 ♗c4 ♖hf8 18 ♖f1 ± Baikov -

Veselovsky, Moscow Ch 1977.
b2) 11 ♘xd5 cd 12 ♗g5
(White may be able to do better with either 12 ♗d2 ♗g7 13 ♗c3 ♕c7 14 0-0-0 ♗e6 15 ♗a6 ♕b6 16 ♗e2, or 12 ♗e3 ♗g7 13 0-0-0 e6 14 ♗d4 ♕e7 15 ♗b5 ♗d7 16 ♗xd7 ♕xd7 17 ♖hf1, Koch - Hartung, Potsdam 1951.) 12 ... h6 (Slightly better is 12 ... ♗e6 13 0-0-0 ♕c7 14 ♗b5, Penrose - Green, Rhyl 1969, though White still has the edge.) 13 ♗h4 g5 14 ♗f2 ♗g7 (Donner - Spanjaard, Holland 1953) 15 ♗d4 ±
11 ♗f4

Black's options here are numerous, but the most important ones are:
B21: 11 ... ♗g7
B22: 11 ... ♗e6

Lesser alternatives are:
B23: 11 ... ♗d7
B24: 11 ... ♗h6
B25: 11 ... g5

B21:

11 ...   ♗g7 (66)

12 0-0-0+ ♗d7!
As to the alternatives:
a) not 12 ... ♕e8?? 13 ♘b5! ♗d7 14 ♘c7+ ♔d8 15 e6 fe 16 ♘xe6+ ♕e8 17 ♘xg7+ ♔f7 18 ♖xd7 ♖hd8 19 ♗c4+ 1-0, Beradze-Akopov, USSR 1966.
b) 12 ... ♕c7 is also bad because of 13 e6+ and now:
b1) 13 ... ♗e5! 14 ♗xe5+ ♘xe5 15 ef with the better ending for White.
b2) 13 ... ♔b7 14 ef ♘f2 15 ♖e1 e5 (if 15 ... ♘xh1 16 ♖xe7+ ♔b6 17 ♘a4+ ♔a5 18 ♗c7+ ♔xa4 19 ♖e4+ with mate to follow.) 16 ♗xe5 ♗xe5 17 ♖xe5 ♘xh1 18 ♖e7+ ♔b6 19 ♘a4+ ♔a5 20 ♖e5+ ♔xa4 21 c3 c5 (on 21 ... ♗e6 22 ♖xe6 ♖ac8 23 ♗a6! ±, or 21 ... a5? 22 ♗d3 mating) 22 ♖xc5 ♗e6 23 ♖c6 ♗c8 24 ♗c4 (threatening 25 ♖c5 with a mating attack) 24 ... ♕a5 25 b4+ ♔a4 26 ♖c5 a5 27 ♔b2 with mate to follow - Boleslavsky.
13 e6
13 ♗e2 is superficial; Black should play:
a) not 13 ... ♘f2 14 ♖xd7+! ♔xd7 15 ♖f1; but
b) 13 ... ♘xe5 14 ♖d4 ♕c7! (not 14 ... h5? 15 ♖hd1 ♗h6 16 g3 followed by ♔b1 ±, nor 14 ... c5 15 ♖d5 ±, nor 14 ... ♕e8 15 ♘e4 ±) 15 ♘e4 =

13 ♖e1 is a less forceful, though still advantageous, alternative: 13 ... g5 14 ♗×g5 (Not 14 ♗g3? h5 ∓) 14 ... ♘×e5 15 ♘e4 ±
15 ... fe
14 ♘e4 e5

The only successful way to meet the threat of 15 ♘c5.

15 ♗e2!

Heidenfeld's recommendation.

If 15 ♗d2 ♗f5! when ... ♘f2 is a real threat; play could continue 16 ♗h6+ ♔c7 17 ♗×g7 ♖hg8 and Black recovers the piece with a good game.

15 ... h5
16 ♗d2! ♗f5

If 16 ... ♔e8 17 h3! ♘f6 (17 ... ♘h6 18 ♘c5! ±) 18 ♗f3 (±) threatens ♘c5.

17 ♗h6+ ♔e8

After 17 ... ♔c7 White wins a piece by 18 ♗×g7 ♖hg8 19 ♗×g4 since he captures the e-pawn with check.

18 ♗×g7 ♖g8
19 ♗f3 ♖×g7
20 h3! ♘e3
21 ♖de1 ♘d5

Not 21 ... ♗×e4? 22 ♗×e4 ♘d5 23 c4 ♘b4 24 a3 winning.

22 ♘g3

White recovers the sacrificed pawn and has a distinct endgame advantage because of Black's horribly split pawns and poor piece co-ordination.

B22:

11 ... ♗e6 (67)

Alexander's suggestion.

12 ♘e4!

This temporary pawn sacrifice is White's best chance.

After **12 h3** ♗h6! 13 ♗×h6 ♘×h6 14 g4 there is:

a) **14 ... ♔c7** 15 0-0-0 f5 16 ef ef 17 ♗g2 f5 = Keres-Padevsky, Moscow 1963.

b) **14 ... f5** 15 ef ef 16 ♗g2 ♔c7.

On 12 0-0-0+ ♔c7 Black has nothing to fear.

12 ... ♗g7

12 ... ♗h6 would now be wrong because of 13 ♗×h6 ♘×h6 and either 14 ♘g5 or 14 ♘c5 giving White an excellent game.

13 ♘c5 ♗×e5

On 13 ... ♘×e5 14 0-0-0+ followed by 15 ♖e1 is very good for White.

14 0-0-0+ ♔c7
15 ♗×e5+ ♘×e5
16 ♘×e6+ fe

17 Re1 &d6
18 g3 ♘g4
19 ♗c4
Not 19 ♗h3 ♘f2 20
R×e6+ &c7 21 ♗g2 ♘×h1
22 R×c6+ &d7 23 ♗×h1
Raf8 with a won game for Black.

19 ... e5
20 Re2

White soon wins the pawn back and maintains a slight but lasting edge. This is not only through the pressure that he can exert against the second black e-pawn, but also because Black has difficulty in finding a reasonable plan, e.g.
a) **10** ... Rhf8 21 Rd1+ &c7 22 ♗e6!
b) **20** ... ♘f6 21 Rd1+ ♘d5 (21 ... &c5 22 R×e5+ &×c4 23 b3+ with mate to follow) 22 Rde1.

B23:
11 ... ♗d7 12 Rd1 ♗g7 (if 12 ... &e8 13 ♗e2 h5 14 ♗f3 ♗g7 15 e6!) 13 e6 ♗×c3+ 14 bc fe 15 ♗e2 Rf8 16 0-0 ♘f6 17 ♗e5 ± - Müller.

B24:
11 ... ♗h6 12 ♗×h6 ♘×h6 13 0-0-0+ (13 ♗e2 ♗g4 14 Rf1 gives White a smaller advantage.) 13 ... &c7 14 ♗c4 and now the following have been tried:

a) **14** ... Rf8 15 h3 ♘f5 16 Rd3 h5 ± Szily-Gadalinski, Poland - Hungary 1949.
b) **14** ... ♗f5 15 h3 g5 16 g4 ♗g6? 17 Rde1! ± Estrin - Kuznetsov, corres 1949.

B25:
11 ... g5 is recommended by Estrin for reducing White's advantage to a minimum, e.g.
a) **12** ♗g3 h5 14 h3 ♘e3 ∓
b) **12** ♗×g5 ♘×e5 13 0-0-0+ &e8 14 h3 when Black's isolated pawns will cause him some trouble but his position is probably tenable.

B3:
8 ... ♘g4 *(68)*
Threatening 9 ... ♕b6.

68
W

9 ♕f3

9 ♗e2 is also quite strong, e.g. 9 ... h5 and now:
a) Not **10** ♗f3? ♕b6 11 ♕e2 ♗a6! 12 ♕e4 d5 13 ♕a4 e6 14 ♘d1 ♗c5 ∓ Birnstein - Hankin, USA 1959.
b) **10 h3** ♘h6 when:
b1) **11 ed** ♕×d6 12 ♗e3

♘f5 13 ♕×d6 ed 14 ♗f2 ♗g7 =.

b2) **11 g4** hg 12 hg ♗g7 13 ed ed = Seidman-Reshevsky, New York 1956.

b3) **11** ♗**e3** ♘f5 12 ♗f2 ♗g7 13 ♗f3 ♕c7 14 ed ed 15 0-0 0-0 16 ♘b5 ♕d7 17 ♘d4 ± Lyublinsky - Aronin, Moscow Ch 1947.

The immediate **9 h3** ♘h6 10 g4, isolating Black's knight, is also playable, e.g. 10 ... f5 11 ef ef 12 ♗g2 d5 13 ♕e2+ ♔f7 14 0-0 ♗c5+ 15 ♔h1 ♖e8 16 ♕f3 ♗a6 17 ♖d1 ± Di Camillo - Henio, US Open 1958.

9 ...   ♕b6

9 ... de 10 ♗b5! and **9 ... d5** 10 ♗d2 followed by 11 0-0-0 both give White an excellent game, but interesting is **9 ... ♗g7 !?** 10 ♗d2 0-0 11 0-0-0 ♖b8 12 ♗c4 ♕b6 13 ♗b3 ½-½, Soltis - Tarjan, Chicago 1973.

10 h3   ♘h6
11 ed   ed
12 g4   ♗g7
13 ♗d2   0-0
14 0-0-0

and White has the better attacking chances.

B4:

8 ...   ♘d7 *(69)*

This is Black's safest reply. Now:

B41: 9 ♗c4

69
W

B42: 9 ♕f3
B43: 9 ed

B41:

9 ♗c4

This is a trappy move, e.g.

a) **9 ... d5?** 10 ♘×d5 cd 11 ♕×d5 ±±.

b) **9 ... de?** 10 0-0 ♕b6+ (10 ... ♗g7 11 ♕f3 ±) 11 ♔h1 ♗g7 12 ♘e4 0-0 13 ♕e2 ef 14 ♗×f4 (threatening 15 ♘g5) 14 ... h6 15 c3 ♘e5 16 ♗×e5 ♗×e5 17 ♘g5! ♗f6 18 ♘×f7! ♔g7 (18 ... ♖×f7? 19 ♖×f6 wins for White) 19 ♘e5 ± Mestrović - Vidmar jnr., Yugoslavia 1951.

Black can secure immediate equality by playing the obvious

9 ...   ♘b6

and now:

a) **10 ed** ♕×d6 (10 ... ♘×c4? 11 ♕d4 ±) 11 ♕×d6 (11 ♗d3 ♗g7 =) 11 ... ed with an equal ending, Averbakh-Lisitsin, 1948.

b) **10** ♗**e2** ♗g7 11 ed ed 12 ♗e3 0-0 13 ♗d4 ♗h6 14 ♕d2 c5 15 ♗f2 ♗b7 16 0-0

11 Levenfish with 6 ... ♞c6

♕f6 17 g3 ♖fe8 18 ♖ad1 ♖ad8 19 a4 ♕f5 20 ♖fe1 ♞xa4! 21 ♗d3 (if 21 ♞xa4 ♕e4) 21 ... ♕c8 22 ♗b5 (22 ♞xa4 ♕c6) 22 ... ♞xc3 23 ♖xe8+ ♖xe8 24 ♕xc3 ♗g7 25 ♕b3 ♖e4 26 ♖xd6 c4 27 ♕a4 ♗f8 28 ♖d7 ♗c5 29 ♖xb7 ♗xf2+ 30 ♔g2 ♗b6 31 ♖d7 ♖e2+ 32 ♔f1 ♖f2+ 33 ♔e1 ♕e8+ 34 0-1, Basman - Jamieson, London 1964. This is an excellent example for revealing the dynamic possibilities at Black's disposal.

B42:

9 ♕f3 *(70)*

70
B

9 ...   ♗g7

a) **9 ... ♕b6?** 10 ed ed 11 ♗e3! ♕xb2 12 ♗d4! ♕xa1+ 13 ♔d2 ♖g8 14 ♕xc6 ♖b8 15 ♗a6 ♕xh1 16 ♗xc8 and White wins. Analysis by Levenfish.

b) **9 ... d5** 10 ♗e3 (10 h4 h5! 11 ♗e3 - *11 e6!? ♞f6 12 ef+ ♔xf7 13 ♗d3 ♗g4 14 ♕f2 ♕b6 = - 11 ... e6 - Also possible is Gufeld's idea 11 ...* ♞b6 followed by ... ♗f5 - *12 g4?! ♖b8 13 gh ♖xh5 - 13 ... ♖xb2? 14 hg fg 15 ♗d3 ± - 14 b3 ♗a3! 15 ♞a4 c5 16 ♕g3 ♗a6! ∓ Nicevski-Ubilava, USSR 1977)* 10 ... ♗g7 (perhaps 10 ... e6, á la Ubilava) 11 ♗d3 0-0 12 0-0 ♞b6 13 a4 d4? 14 a5 de 15 ab ♕xb6 16 ♔h1 and 17 ♞a4 with advantage to White — Levenfish.

10 ♗b5

The greedy **10 ♕xc6** is bad on account of 10 ... ♖b8 11 ed (11 ♗e3 could transpose into the next note) 11 ... 0-0 12 ♗e2 ♗b7 13 ♕c7 ♗xg2 14 ♕xd8 ♖fxd8 15 de ♖e8 16 ♖g1 ♗c6 when Black has ample compensation for the pawn.

10 ♗e3 is also weak. Black can continue forcefully: 10 ... 0-0 11 ♕xc6 ♖b8 12 0-0-0 de 13 ♗xa7 ♖b7 14 ♕a4 ef 15 ♞b5 ♞b6 16 ♕b3 ♕e8 and Black won quickly — Shaposhnikov - Bonch-Osmolovsky, 20th USSR Ch 1952.

After 10 ♗b5 Black has:
B421: 10 ... ♖b8
B422: 10 ... 0-0
10 ... de 11 ♗xc6 ♖b8 transposes into B421.

B421:

10 ... ♖b8 11 ♗xc6 de 12 ♗e3 ♖xb2 13 0-0-0 e4! 14 ♕xe4 (not 14 ♞xe4?

♕a5 etc.) 14 ... ♗×c3 15 ♗×d7+ ♗×d7 16 ♖×d7 ♕×d7 17 ♕a8+ *(71)*

71 B

17 ...   ♖b8!!

This strange move is actually forced. In Shaposhnikov — Bonch-Osmoslovsky, USSR 1958, Black played 17 ... ♕d8 and resigned after 18 ♕c6+ ♕d7 19 ♕×c3.

18 ♕×b8+ ♕d8 19 ♕×d8+ ♔×d8 20 ♗×a7 ♔c7 21 ♗c5 ♖a8 22 a3 ♔c6 23 ♗×e7 ♖a7 ½-½ Grägger-Honfi, Austria - Hungary 1961.

B422:

10 ... 0-0 worked out quite well in Bronstein - Vasyukov, 26th USSR Ch 1959, viz. 11 ♕×c6 ♖b8 12 ♗e3 a6 13 ♗a4 de 14 0-0-0 ♕a5 15 ♗b3 ef 16 ♗×f4 ♖×b3 17 ab ♕a1+ 18 ♔d2 ♕×b2 19 ♖b1 ♘b8! 20 ♕×c8 (20 ♖×b2? ♖d8+) 20 ... ♖×c8 21 ♖×b2 ♗×c3+ 22 ♔c1 ♗×b2+ 23 ♔×b2 when Black's extra pawn is not worth very much because of White's ♕-side majority (½-½, 33 moves).

B43:

9 ed   ed *(72)*

72 W

10 ♗e3

This move, threatening 11 ♗d4, is the only way for White to play for an advantage.

Alternatives are:

a) **10 ♕e2+** and now:

a1) **10 ... ♗e7** 11 ♖e3 (not **11 b3?** 0-0 12 ♗b2 ♗h4+, nor **11 g3** 0-0 12 ♗g2 d5 $\mp$) 11 ... 0-0 12 0-0-0 ♘f6 13 h3 ♗e6 14 g4 ♕a5 15 ♕a6 ♕×a6 16 ♗×a6 ♘d5 17 ♘×d5 ♗×d5 18 ♖×d5! cd 19 ♖d1 ♗d8 (if 19 ... ♗f6 20 ♖×d5 ♖fe8 21 ♗d2 ♖ad8 22 ♗d3 ±) 20 ♖×d6 ♗b6 21 ♗d2 ♖ad8 22 ♗b5 f6 23 a4 ♖f7 24 a5 ±, Martsum - Neishtadt, corres 1959.

a2) **10 ... ♕e7** 11 ♘e4 ♕e6! 12 ♗d2 ♗e7 13 ♗c3 0-0 14 g3 d5 15 ♘f2 ♗f6 = Koblencs.

b) **10 ♕d4** and now:

b1) **10 ... ♕f6** 11 ♗e3 ♗g7

12 0-0-0 and now both 12 ... d5 13 ♕×f6 ♗×f6 14 ♘a4 (or 14 ♗d4) and 12 ... ♕×d4 13 ♗×d4 14 ♖×d4 d5 15 ♘a4 are slightly better for White.
b2) **10 ... ♘f6** when:
b21) **11 b3?!** is a dubious attempt to kill Black on the long diagonal. Timman-Langeweg, Amsterdam 1974, continued 11 ... ♗g7 12 ♗b2 0-0 13 0-0-0 ♗g4! 14 ♗e2?! ♘d5 and White had nothing better than 15 ♕×g7+ ♔×g7 16 ♘×d5+ f6 17 ♗×g4!? cd and the bishop pair was no match for Black's queen. However, c22) **11 ♗e3** allows Black a good game with 11 ... ♗e7! 12 ♗e2 0-0 13 0-0 c5 (Or Langeweg's 13 ... ♘g4) 14 ♕d2 d5 15 ♗f3 ♗b7 16 ♖ad1 ♖b8 = Szabo - Reshevsky, Helsinki OL 1952.
c) **10 ♗e2 ♘f6 11 ♗e3 ♗g7 12 ♗f3 0-0! 13 ♗×c6 ♖b8 14 0-0 ♖×b2 15 ♗d4 ♕a5 16 ♘e4 ♘×e4 17 ♗×g7 ♔×g7 18 ♕d4+ ♘f6 19 ♕×b2 ♕c5+ 20 ♔h1 ♕×c6** ∓

After 10 ♗e3 Black has two main alternatives:
B431: 10 ... ♗e7
B432: 10 ... ♕e7

The other alternatives are not particularly attractive:
a) **10 ... ♘f6?** 11 ♕d2 ♗g7 12 0-0 d5 13 ♗c5 ±

b) **10 ... d5?** 11 ♗d4 ♘f6 12 ♕e2+ ♗e6 13 f5 ±.

B431:
10 ...   ♗e7 (73)

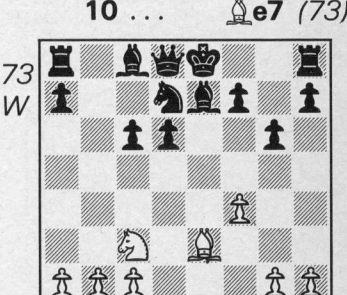

73
W

11 ♕f3

11 ♕d2 has been given a new lease of life by Larsen, but it is unlikely that it represents a serious threat to 10 ... ♗e7. After **11 ... 0-0** 12 0-0-0, Larsen-Lein, Lone Pine 1979 continued **12 ... ♘b6** (12 ... ♕a5 13 ♔b1 d5 14 f5 ♗f6 15 ♗d4 ♗×d4 16 ♕×d4 ♖b8 17 ♕d2 ♘c5, Scherbakov - Lisitsin, 22nd USSR Ch 1955, reaches a critical position with the outlook probably good for Black.)

(Yet another plausible possibility is **12 ... d5** at once, e.g. 13 ♘a4? ♖b8 14 ♕c3 ♕c7, with attacking prospects.) 13 ♗e2 d5 14 h4 h5 15 g4! ♗×g4 16 ♗×g4 ♘c4 17 ♕d3 ♕b8 18 b3 ♗a3+ 19 ♔b1 ♖e8 20 ♗d4 ♘b2 21 ♕d2 hg 22 f5 ♘×d1 23 ♕h6 ±±.

Also insufficient is **12 ... ♘f6?!** 13 h3 ♗e6 14 g4, with good attacking prospects for White, Fuderer - Trifunović, Yugoslav Ch 1953, but Black can improve earlier with **11 ... ♘f6!**, preserving the option of which side to castle. Honfi - Partos, Bucharest 1973, continued: 12 0-0-0 ♗e6 13 ♗d3 ♕a5 ∞ 14 f5!? gf 15 ♗d4 ♖g8 16 ♕e2 ♖g4! 17 ♗c4 d5 18 ♕e5 0-0-0 ∓.

11 ... d5
12 0-0-0 ♗f6

In Tarjan - Timman, Venice 1974, Black played 12 ... 0-0 immediately, when White overreacted with 13 g4?! and after 13 ... ♗f6 14 ♗d4 ♗×d4 15 ♖×d4 ♖b8 16 ♖d2 ♕b6 ∓ Black had the better attacking prospects.

13 ♗d4   0-0
14 h4   ♖b8
15 ♕f2   ♖b4
16 ♗×f6 ♘×f6
17 a3   ♖b7 =

- Geller.

Black should keep queens on to preserve the possibility of a counter attack. After 17 ... ♕b6 18 ♕×b6 ♖×b6 19 ♘a4 ± Black was steadily mown down in Tal-Lisitsin, 23rd USSR Ch 1956.

B432:
10 ...   ♕e7 *(74)*
This, in conjunction with

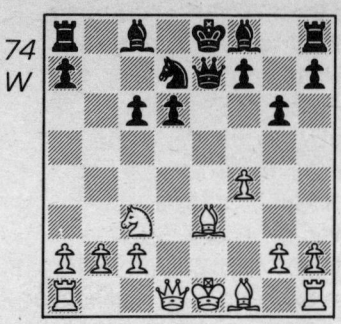
74
W

Black's next move, is Eliskases' resource.

11 ♕d4

11 ♕d2 is innocuous, Black being able to equalise without difficulty by 11 ... ♗g7 12 0-0-0 0-0 13 ♗d4 (not 13 ♖e1 ♘f6 14 ♗c5 ♕b7 15 ♗×d6 ♖d8 16 ♖e7 ♗d7 17 ♗e5 ♕b4 18 ♗×f6 ♗f5 19 ♖b7 ♖×d2 with a won game for Black, Nielson - Coolen, corres 1958) 13 ... ♗×d4 14 ♕×d4 d5 15 ♗d3 (if 15 ♗e2 ♖b8 16 a3 ♘c5 17 ♖he1 ♗f5 18 ♗f3 ♕b7 ∓) 15 ... ♖b8 =

11 ...   ♗g7!

Not 11 ... ♘f6? 12 0-0-0 ♗g7 13 ♕×d6 ♕×e3+ 14 ♔b1 ±, e.g.: 14 ... ♘d7 15 ♗a6 ♗×c3 16 ♗×c8 ♖×c8 17 ♕×d7+ ♔f8 18 ♕×c8+ ♔g7 19 ♕c7 ♗f6 20 ♖d7 ±± Orekhov - Goloborodko, Odessa 1973.

12 ♕×g7 ♕×e3+
13 ♗e2

13 ♔d1 fails to 13 ... ♖f8 14 ♗b5 ♘e5! 15 fe cb with

the threat of 16 ... ♗g4+.
13 ♘e2 ♖f8 **14** ♖d1 only leads to equality, e.g.
a) Black must not play **14 ... ♘c5?** because of 15 ♖×d6 ♘e4 16 ♖d8+ ♔×d8 17 ♕×f8+ ♔c7 18 ♕e7+! followed by a check at b4 or e5 followed by 20 ♕d4 forcing the exchange of queens and thus securing a won ending.
b) **14 ... ♗a6** (an idea of Vuković's) gives White a slight endgame advantage after 15 ♕d4 (15 ♖×d6 only leads to equality after 15 ... ♗×e2 16 ♗×e2 ♕×f4 17 ♕d4 ♕×d4 18 ♖×d4 0-0-0.) 15 ... ♕×d4 16 ♘×d4 ♗×f1 17 ♖×f1.
c) **14 ... d5** (best) 15 ♖d3 ♕b6! (not 15 ... ♕e7 16 ♕c3! when Black is in some difficulty) 16 ♘d4 ♘c5 17 ♖e3+ ♗e6 18 ♗d3 0-0-0 19 0-0 20 ♔h6 ♗d7 = Secular-Bruggemann, corres 1959.

13 ...   ♖f8
14 ♖f1 *(75)*

14 ♖d1 is met adequately by

14 ... ♗a6.
Black must now play as actively as possible.
14 ...   ♗a6

Müller's suggestion of **14 ... ♔d8** leads to equality if White fails to find the most aggressive continuation and plays **15 ♖d1** ♔c7 16 ♖f3 (16 f5 or 16 ♕×h7 can be met by 16 ... ♗a6) 16 ... ♕g1+ 17 ♖f1 ♕e3 etc.

Grave doubts, however, have been raised by a recent game in which White played **15 ♖f3!** ♕g1+ (if 15 ... ♕b6 16 0-0-0 ± - Ciocaltea.) 16 ♗f1 ♖e8+ 17 ♘e2 ♗a6 18 0-0-0! ♗×e2 19 ♗×e2 ♕×g2 20 ♖fd3! ♕×e2 (or 20 ... ♖×e2 21 ♖×d6 ♖×c2+ 22 ♔b1 ♖×b2+ 23 ♕×b2 ♕×b2+ 24 ♔×b2 ♖b8+ 25 ♔c2 ♖b7 26 ♖×c6 ± - Ciocaltea.) 21 ♖×d6 ♕e7 (not 21 ... ♖e7? 22 ♕f8+) 22 ♖×d7+ ♕×d7 23 ♕×f7! ♕×d1+ 24 ♔×d1 Urzica - Vujačić, Stockholm 1969.

14 ... ♘c5 15 ♖d1 d5 16 ♖f3 also lands Black in hot water, e.g.:
a) **16 ... ♕e7** 17 ♕d4 f5 18 ♔f1! ♖b8 19 a3 ±.
b) **16 ... ♕g1+** 17 ♔d2 ♕×h2 (if 17 ... ♕×g2 18 ♖e3+ ♗e6 19 ♕d4 ♘d7 20 ♕a4 c5 21 ♔c1 ±) 18 ♘×d5

and now:

b1) **18 ...** ♘e4+ 19 ♔c1 cd 20 ♕e5+ ♗e6 21 ♕c7! ♖d8 22 ♗b5+ ♖d7 23 ♗×d7+ ♗×d7 24 ♖×d5 wins for White.

b2) **18 ... cd** 19 ♗b5+ ♗d7 20 ♖e3+ ♘e4+ 21 ♖×e4+ de 22 ♕e5+ ♔d8 23 ♔c1 and White wins.

14 ... ♖b8 is also met by 15 ♖f3, e.g.: 15 ... ♕e7 (if **15 ...** ♕g1+ 16 ♗f1 ♖×b2 17 0-0-0 ♕b6 18 ♖×d6; or **15 ...** ♕b6 16 b3) 16 ♕d4 ♘c5 17 0-0-0 d5 18 ♖e3 ♗e6 19 g4 ♖b4 (if 19 ... f5 20 gf ♖×f5 21 ♗g4 ♖f6 22 a3) 20 ♕g7 ♖×f4 (if **20 ...** ♕c7 21 f5; or **20 ... f5** 21 ♕×e7+ ♔×e7 22 ♖×d5) 21 ♘×d5! cd 22 ♗b5+ ♔d8 23 ♖×d5+ ♗×d5 24 ♖×e7 ♔×e7 25 ♕e5+ ♘e6 26 ♕×d5 ± Kizov - Ilievsky, Macedonian Ch 1972.

15 ♖f3!? ♕g1+
On 15 ... ♕e7 16 ♔d2! (threatening 17 ♖e3) is very strong.
16 ♗f1!
16 ♔d2 ♕×a1 17 ♗×a6 ♕×b2 does not give White any real chance to find compensation for his material deficit.

At one time it was thought that White would have the worst of the struggle here unless he took the draw by 16 ♖f1 ♕e3 17 ♖f3, but, as will be shown, this is not really the case.

16 ... ♗×f1
17 0-0-0 ♕×g2?
The correct order of moves, transposing into the game, is

17 ... 0-0-0 18 ♖d×f1 ♕×g2
18 ♖d×f1?
Missing **18** ♖e3+ ♔d8 19 ♖×d6 ♔c7 20 ♕d4 ♖fd8 21 ♖e7 ♕g4 22 ♕e5! ♔b7 23 ♘a4! with a devastating attack.
18 ♖e1+ ♔d8 19 ♖d×f1 is quite different, since the black king will be quite safe on c7.
18 ... 0-0-0
19 ♘e4?
Public opinion on this variation was misled by the fact of Black's victory in the game Unzicker - Kottnauer, Leysin 1967, and by the notes to that game written by Kottnauer and Hartston in 1967 and endorsed shortly afterwards by Marić in Informator 4.

Unzicker - Kottnauer continued, after **19** ♘e4?, with 19 ... ♘c5 20 ♘×d6+ (if **20** ♘×c5 dc Black threatens 21 ... ♕d2+. **20** ♘g5 would have been best.) 20 ... ♖×d6! 21 ♖3f2 (on 21 ♕×f8+ ♖d8 Black threatens 22 ... ♕d2+ with mate to follow.) 21 ... ♕d5 22 ♕×f8+ ♖d8 23

♕g7? (After this White is certainly losing. Relatively best is 23 ♕h6 ♘e4! 24 ♕h3+ f5 25 ♕b3 ♕×b3 26 ab ♘×f2 27 ♖×f2 ♖d4 28 c3 ♖e4 when Black has distinctly the better of the rook and pawn ending as White can never exchange rooks.) 23 ... ♕×a2 24 b3 ♘e4! 25 ♕b2 ♕×b2+ 26 ♔×b2 ♘×f2 27 ♖×f2 ♖d5 28 ♖e2 ♔d7 29 ♔c3 ♔d6 30 ♖e8 a5 31 ♖e4 ♖h5 32 ♖d4+ ♔c5 0-1. (Both 33 ♖d2 ♖h3+ 34 ♔b2 ♖f3 and 33 ♖d7 ♖h3+ 34 ♔b2 f5 35 ♖d2 ♖h4 36 ♖f2 ♔d4 are without hope.)

Correct perspective has been restored to this line by Ciocaltea, who recommended **19 ♕d4!** ♘b6 20 h3 *(76)* (to take away the flight square g4 from the black queen).

76
B

This was successfully tried out in a game won by the Rumanian lady player, Nicolau, against Georgieva at Gori 1970; that game continued **20 ... ♖fe8** 21 ♕d3 c5 22 ♕d1 ♘c4 23 ♖1f2 ♘e3 24 ♖×g2 ♘×g2 25 ♕d5 1-0.

Let us now return to the position arising after Ciocaltea's 20 h3 *(76)* and attempt to reach a balanced verdict on this, which the author considers typical of the problems of the Levenfish.

It may be of value to appraise the general positional features of this situation before engaging in an investigation of precise concrete variations:

In Black's favour are the following factors:

a) The slight weakness of White's back rank.
b) White's K-side pawns are a serious endgame liability.
c) Black's pieces are all developed.
d) Black has an extra pawn.

To offset Black's assets is the fact that Black's pieces, although developed, do not co-operate; they are cut off in isolated detachments; the queen especially is in danger of being trapped and White can exploit this to organise a dual attack on the black queen and the key points c6 and a7. White is well developed and his centralised forces are ideally placed for action on both wings.

Now to examine some concrete variations:

The main danger for Black is that his king will be dissected while he is seeking to extricate his queen. As can be seen from Nicolau-Georgieva, Black's first priority is to release his queen from the death trap on g2. Since 20 ... ♖fe8 fails, there is no alternative but to resort to **20 ... g5(!)** - suggested by the author - hoping to provide an avenue of escape for the queen along the g-file or the b8-h2 diagonal. After 20 ... g5 White has two forceful continuations in **21 a4** and **21 f5** which lead to complications, and the simple 21 ♕e4 guaranteeing White a great endgame advantage, e.g.:

a) **21 ... ♔b7** 22 ♕e7+ and 23 ♕×g5

b) **21 ... d5** 22 ♕f5+ ♔b8(!) 23 ♕×g5 ♕×g5 24 fg ♖d7 25 h4 ♘c4 (or 25 ... ♖e7 26 ♖f6) 26 ♘a4 and Black's position is every bit as bad as it looks - analysis by Keene.

This analysis bears out our contention that White has the advantage after 20 h3. The best that Black can hope for is an inferior ending.

12 Levenfish with 6 ... ♗g7!

1 e4 c5 2 ♘f3 d6 3 d4 cd 4 ♘×d4 ♘f6 5 ♘c3 g6 6 f4 6 ... ♗g7! *(77)*

77
W

This move is the very response that the Levenfish Attack was designed to refute, and until very recently it was considered almost insane for Black to reply with the routine development of his KB. But times change.

In July 1974 the move 6 ... ♗g7 was revived, quite independently, by Mestel and myself. I believe that I was the first, by a few days when I essayed the move against Lennox in the Scottish Championship at Ayr, though Mestel's victory over Vladimirov was more dramatic.

Our new idea, though Mestel did not actually get the chance to test it, was to employ an innovation given by Trifunovic as an equalising line. This new move revived a position considered by theory to be hopeless for Black.

7 e5! *(78)*

78
B

The most consistent continuation.

After 7 ♗b5+ ♘fd7! 8 ♗e3 0-0 9 ♗e2 ♘c6 Black's position is quite comfortable, e.g. 1) **10 ♘b3** ♘b6 11 0-0 ♗e6 12 ♔h1 ♘c4 14 ♗c1 b5! ∓ Szily-Gereben, Hungary 1948. b) **10 0-0** ♘b6! 11 ♘d5 ♗×d4 =

From the diagram Black has

12 Levenfish with 6... ♗g7!

tried several moves:
A: 7... ♘fd7
B: 7... ♘g4
C: 7... ♘g8
D: 7... ♗g4
E: 7... de
F: 7... ♘h5

A:

7... **♘fd7?** 8 e6! ♘f6 9 ef+ ♔xf7 10 ♗c4+ d5 11 ♗b3 ♖f8 12 ♕f3 e6 13 ♗e3 ♔g8 14 0-0-0 to be followed by a K-side pawn storm (±).

B:

7...   ♘g4
8 ♗b5+ ♔f8
If 8... ♗d7 9 ♕xg4
9 h3   ♘h6

10 ♗e3 ♘c6 11 ed ♘xd4 12 ♗xd4 ♕xd6 13 ♗xg7+ ♔xg7 14 ♕xd6 ed 15 0-0-0. In the original game of this attack, Levenfish - Rabinovich, 11th USSR Ch 1939, White now won the Black d-pawn and eventually the ending: 15... ♖d8 16 ♖d2 ♗e6 17 ♖hd1 ♘f5 18 g4 ♘e3 19 ♖e1 a6 (If 19... ♘c4 20 ♗xc4 ♗xc4 21 ♖ed1 and White wins the d-pawn at once.) 20 ♖xe3 ab 21 ♘xb5 ♖xa2 22 ♖xd6 ♖xd6 23 ♘xd6 ♖a1+ 24 ♔d2 ♖f1 25 ♘xb7 ♖xf4 26 ♘c5 ♗d5 27 ♘d3 ♖f1 28 b3 ♔h6 29 c4 ♗g2 30 ♔e2 ♖b1 31 g5+! ♔g7 32 ♔f2 ♗b7 33 b4 ♗c8 34 c5 ♗f5

35 c6! h6 (35... ♗xd3 36 ♖xd3 ♖xb4 37 c7 ♖c4 38 ♖d7 wins.) 36 gh+ ♔xh6 37 c7 ♖b3 38 h4 ♖c3 39 ♘c5 ♖c4 40 ♖e5! ♗g4 41 ♖e4 ♖c2+ 42 ♔e3 ♗f5 43 ♖f4 ♖c8 44 ♖xf7 ♖c4 45 ♖f4 1-0.

C:

7... ♘g8 8 ♗b5+ ♔f8 (8... ♗d7 9 e6 ±) 9 0-0 d5 (9... de?? 10 ♘e6+) 10 ♗e3 a6 11 ♗e2 e6 (if 11... b5? 12 ♘xd5!) 12 ♘e4! ♘c6 (12... de? 13 ♘xe6+) 13 ♘xc6 bc 14 ♗c5+ ♘e7 15 ♘f6 ± Rellstab-Wittenberg, Hamburg 1950.

D:

7... ♗g4 8 ♗b5+! ♔f8 (if 8... ♘c6 9 ef ♗xd1 10 fg ♖g8 11 ♘xc6 winning, or 8... ♘bd7 9 ♕d3! ±) 9 ♕d3 ♘e8 10 0-0 ♘d7 (10... de?? 11 ♘e6+) 11 h3 de 12 fe ♘xe5 13 hg! ♘c7 (If 13... ♘xd3 14 ♘e6+ wins a piece.) 14 ♕e4 ♕xd4+ 15 ♕xd4 ♘f3+ 16 ♖xf3 ♗xd4+ 17 ♗e3 ♗xc3 18 ♗c4 ♗f6 19 g5 winning, Koch - Nüsken, Grethen 1950.

E:

7... **de!**
The least unpleasant of Black's options.
8 fe

12 Levenfish with 6 ... ♗g7!

and now:
E1: 8 ... ♘g8
E2: 8 ... ♘h5
E3: 8 ... ♘d5
E4: 8 ... ♘g4
E5: 8 ... ♘fd7!

E1:
8 ... ♘**g8** 9 ♗b5+ ♗d7 10 e6! ♗×b5 11 ♘c×b5 ♘f6 12 ♕f3 ♕b6 13 ef+ ♔×f7 14 ♕b3+ e6 15 ♘c7! ♕×c7 16 ♕×e6+ ♔f8 17 ♕×f6+! ♗×f6 18 ♘e6+ winning, Vlagsma - Wind, Rotterdam 1946.

E2:
8 ... ♘**h5??** 9 ♗b5+ ♗d7 10 g4 winning a piece.

E3:
8 ... ♘**d5** 9 ♗b5+ ♔f8 10 0-0 ♗×e5 (10 ... e6 11 ♕f3) 11 ♗h6+ ♔g8 (11 ... ♗g7 12 ♗×g7+ ♔×g7 13 ♘×d5 wins material.) 12 ♘×d5 ♕×d5 13 ♘f5! ♕c5+ 14 ♗e3 ♕c7 15 ♘h6+ ♔g7 16 ♖×f7++, Schwarz - Marquardt, Berlin 1950.

E4:
8 ... ♘**g4**
9 ♗b5+ ♘c6
9 ... ♔f8?? 10 ♗e6+ 1-0 actually happened in Eales - de Veauce, Paignton 1968 and countless other games.
10 ♘×c6 ♕×d1+ 11 ♘×d1
11 ♔×d1 ♘f2+ 12 ♔e2 ♘×h1 13 ♘d4+ and 14 ♗f4 gives White two minor pieces for a rook and is therefore equally convincing.
11 ...   a6
12 ♗a4   ♗d7
13 h3   ♘h6
Not 13 ... ♘×e5 14 ♘×e5
14 ♘×e7 (79)

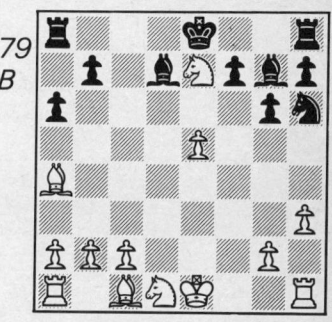

14 ...   ♗×a4
After 14 ... ♔×e7 15 ♗g5+ ♔e8 16 ♗×d7+ ♔×d7 17 0-0 Black would have been clearly lost.
15 ♘d5   ♖d8
16 c4   ♘f5
If 16 ... ♗×d1 17 ♖×d1 b5 (17 ... 0-0 18 ♗g5 ♖d7 19 ♔f2 ±) 18 ♗g5! is also very good for White.
17 ♗g5   ♖d7
18 ♘1c3 ♗c6 19 0-0-0 h5 20 ♘c7+ ♔f8 21 ♖×d7 ♗×d7 22 ♖d1 ♗×e5 23 ♖×d7 h4 24 ♘e4 ♘d4 25 ♖d8+ ♔g7 26 ♘e8+ ♔h7 27 ♘4f6+ ♗×f6+ 28 ♘×f6+ 1-0 Pilnik-Kashdan, New York 1949.

E5:

8 ... ♘fd7 !

Relatively best.

9 e6 *(80)*

9 ... ♘e5

There is nothing better. If 9 ... fe 10 ♘×e6 ♗×c3+ 11 bc ♕b6 12 ♗c4 ♘f6 13 ♖b1!! ♕×b1 14 ♘c7+ ♔f8 15 ♕d8+ ♘e8 16 ♕×e8+ ♔g7 17 ♕f7++ - Schwarz.

10 ♗b5+ ♘bc6
11 ef+ ♔×f7
12 0-0+ ♗f6
13 ♘×c6

If 13 ♗×c6 ♘×c6 14 ♘×c6 ♕×d1 15 ♘×d1 bc 16 ♗g5 as recommended by Koblencs, 16 ... ♗f5 17 ♗×f6 ef 18 ♘e3 ♗e6 gives a tenable ending - Gufeld.

13 ... bc

Or 13 ... ♘×c6 14 ♘d5! 14 ♕×d8

Not 14 ♗f4 ♔g7! (After 14 ... ♕b6+ 15 ♔h1 White gains the advantage in Kamishov - Averbakh, Moscow teams Ch 1948.) 15 ♗×e5 ♗×e5 16 ♕×d8 ♖×d8 17 ♗×c6 ♖b8 with a balanced position.

14 ... ♖×d8
15 ♗a4

with some advantage to White according to Boleslavsky; but 15 ... ♔g7, as in the previous note, may give Black a playable position.

F:

7 ... ♘h5 *(81)*

8 ♗b5+

Not 8 g4?? ♘×f4 9 ♗×f4 d×e5 ∓∓.

8 ... ♗d7
9 e6

9 ♕f3?! was played in Vladimirov-Mestel, World Cadet Ch Pont Sainte Maxence 1974: 9 ... de 10 fe ♗×e5 11 ♘e3 (11 ♕×b7 ♗×d4 12 ♕×a8 ♗×c3+ ∓∓) 11 ... ♗×b5 12 ♘c×b5 (or 12 ♘d×b5 ♘c6 and Black is a safe pawn up) 12 ... ♕a5+!? (12 ... ♕d7 13 0-0-0 0-0 is simpler) 13 c3 (13 b4 ♕b6!) 13 ... a6! 14 ♕d5 (14 ♘a3 ♕c7 leaves the knight hopelessly placed: 14 ♕×b7 ab 15 b4

12 Levenfish with 6 ... ♗g7!

♕a6) 14 ... ♗×d4! 15 ♘d6+ (or 15 ♗×d4 0-0! 16 ♕e5 f6 ∓∓) 15 ... ed 16 ♕×a5 ♗×e3 (Black is probably winning. Even if White succeeds in sorting out his king and rooks, Black plays ... d5-d4 and centralises his pieces.) 17 ♔d1 ♘c6 18 ♕c7 0-0 19 ♖f1 ♖ab8 20 ♔c2 ♘d4+! 21 ♔b1 (if 21 ♔d3 ♘f4+! 22 ♖×f4 ♘e6! 23 ♕×b8 ♘×f4+ 24 ♔×e3 ♘×g2+ wins comfortably) 21 ... ♘e6 22 ♕×d6 ♖bd8 23 ♕e7 ♖d2 24 a3 ♘hf4 25 ♕×b7 ♘c5 26 ♕f3 ♘d5 0-1. White is faced with the threat of 27 ... ♘×c3+. If 27 ♖c1 ♘d3 28 ♖c2 ♘×c3+ mates. (Notes by Mestel.)

9 ... fe

Not 9 ... ♗×b5 10 ef+ ♔×f7 11 ♘d×b5 ♘f6 12 0-0, threatening 13 f5 ± Levenfish.

10 ♘×e6 ♗×c3+
11 bc ♕c8! (82)

82
W

This is Trifunović's improvement over the older continuation 11 ... ♕a5 12 ♗d2! ♗×b5 13 c4! ±. Strangely, or perhaps not, the text is not mentioned by Geller in *Encyclopaedia of Chess Openings*.

12 ♕d3

12 ♗×**d7**+ ♘×d7 (12 ... ♔×d7? 13 ♘g5 ♕c4 14 ♖b1 ♔c7 15 ♖b4 ♕×a2 16 ♕e2 ♘c6 17 ♘e6+ 1-0 J. Littlewood - Mestel, British Ch 1979; If 17 ... ♔c8 18 ♖×b7! wins) 13 0-0 ♘hf6 14 ♕e2 ♘f5 15 ♕b5+ ♘fd7 16 ♘d4 ♘e4 17 ♖e1 a6 18 ♕e2 ♘df6 19 c4 0-0 ∓ 20 ♔h1 ♕g4 21 ♕×g4 ♘×g4 22 ♔g1 ♘fg6 23 g43 ♘c5 24 ♖×e7 ♖ae8 25 ♖×e8 ♖×e8 26 h3 ♖e4 27 ♘b3 ♖×c4 28 ♗b2 ♘fe4 29 ♘×c5 ♘×c5 30 ♖d1 ♖×c2 31 ♗a3 ♖×a2 32 ♗×c5 dc ∓∓ Lennox - Levy, Scottish Ch 1974.

12 ♕**d4** ♘f6 13 ♕c4 ♘c6 14 ♘d4 ♘×d4 15 cd (15 ♗×d7+ ♕×d7 16 cd - 16 ♕×d4 ♕e6+ ∓ - 16 ... ♖c8 ∓) 15 ... ♕×c4 16 ♗×c4 ♗f5! ∓ MacHack - Levy, Cambridge (Mass.) 1978.

12 ... ♗×b5
13 ♕×b5+ ♘c6
14 ♘g5 h6
15 ♘f3 ♕f5
16 ♕×b7 ♕e4+
17 ♔f2 ♖b8! =

Clearly Trifunović's equality sign is, to say the least, simplifying the issue.

Much experience will be required to determine whether Black's freedom of movement compensates for his poor pawn structure. Just to confuse the issue still further, I should perhaps mention that Tatai prefers White, Keene prefers Black, and I wouldn't like to play the position with either colour!

Seriously though, if White can find time for the advance f5 I feel that he will have good attacking chances. Otherwise I would prefer Black.

Index of Variations

1 e4 c5 2 ♘f3 d6 3 d4 cd 4 ♘×d4 ♘f6 5 ♘c3 g6
6 h3	2
6 ♘de2	3
6 ♗b5+	3
6 ♘d5	4
6 ♗g5	4
6 g3	5

Classical 6 ♗e2

6 ♗e2 ♗g7 7 ♘b3	9
7 ♗e3 ♘c6 8 ♘b3 0-0 9 f4 ♗e6	16
9 ... a5	21
9 ... ♘a5	22
9 ... e5	23
8 ♕d2 0-0 9 ♘b3	25
9 0-0-0	25
9 0-0 ♗d7	27
9 ... a6	28
9 ... d5	29
9 ... ♘g4	33
10 ♗×g4 ♗×g4 11 f4	34
11 ♘d5	36
11 ♘×c6	37
11 h3	37
11 f3	37
8 g4?	38
8 h3	38
8 f3	39
8 h4	39
8 0-0 Miscellaneous	41

6 ♗e2 ♗g7 7 0-0 ♘c6 8 ♘b3 0-0 9 ♗g5 ♗e6 — 43
                                                  9 ... a5 — 46
                                                  9 ... a6 — 47
6 ♗e2 ♗g7 7 ♗e3 ♘c6 8 0-0 0-0 9 h3 — 49
                                                  9 f3 — 50
                                                  9 ♔h1 — 50
                                                  9 f4 ♕b6 10 ♕d3 — 51
                                                                     10 e5 — 52
                                                  9 ♘b3 ♗d7 — 55
                                                  9 ... a5 — 55
                                                9 ... ♗e6 10 h3 — 58
                                                                     10 f3 — 58
                      10 f4 ♘a5 11 f5 ♗c4 12 fg — 62
                                                                 12 g4 — 62
                                                                 12 ♘×a5 — 62
                                                                 12 ♗d3 — 66
                                                                 12 ♔h1 — 68
                      10 f4 ♕c8 11 ♔h1 — 69
                                          11 ♕d2 — 71
                                          11 ♕e1 — 71
                                          11 h3 — 72

Levenfish 6 f4
6 f4 ♘bd7 — 78
6 ... ♘c6 7 ♗b5 — 84
              7 ♘×c6 bc 8 e5 ♗g4 — 90
                      8 ... de — 90
                      8 ... ♘g4 — 93
                      8 ... ♘d7 — 94
6 ... ♗g7 7 e5 ♘fd7 — 104
           7 ... ♘g4 — 104
           7 ... ♘g8 — 104
           7 ... ♗g4 — 104
           7 ... de — 104
           7 ... ♘h5 — 106

Index of Complete Games

Alekhine-Botvinnik	19
Basman-Jamieson	95
Benko-Wexler	43
Beradze-Akopov	91
Eales-de Veauce	105
Estrin-Veresov	21
Filipowicz-Hollis	66
Fink-Estrin	77
Fischer-Reshevsky	20
Foltys-Eliskases	17
Grechkin-Saigin	25
Gusev-Averbakh	11
Holmov-Aronin	70
Keres-Gligoric	8
Korchnoi-Spassky	79
Kramar-Kovalyev	19
Lasker-Napier	3
Levenfish-Rabinovich	104
J.Littlewood-Mestel	107
Nei-Pitksaar	20
Nicolau-Georgieva	101
Penrose-Barden	90
Pilnik-Kashdan	105
Rauzer-Botvinnik	61
Rauzer-Kan	5
Richter-Petrow	34
Rolland-Larsen	75
Salhaarzhuren-Stein	39
Samarian-Roele	54
Schories-Koch	18

Smyslov-Botvinnik   40, 40, 41
Smyslov-Geller   49
Smyslov-Korchnoi   10
Soltis-Tarjan   94
Spielmann-Alekhine   57
Tuomainen-Lee   80
Unzicker-Kottnauer   100
van den Berg-Larsen   13
van Hombeek-Nikitin   76
Vladimirov-Mestel   106
Wach-Oley   51